Twenty Years at Sea

THE WORLD AS MY CLASSROOM

Laura Goor

 FriesenPress

Suite 300 - 990 Fort St
Victoria, BC, V8V 3K2
Canada

www.friesenpress.com

ISBN
978-1-5255-7567-9 (Hardcover)
978-1-5255-7568-6 (Paperback)
978-1-5255-7569-3 (eBook)

1. *Travel, Special Interest, Adventure*
2. *Cruising, Inspirational, Personal Growth*

Distributed to the trade by The Ingram Book Company

Table of Contents

The World is my Passion!

⟋⟍

For all the incredible people who touched my life throughout my personal journey *and* to all those individuals who currently bless my life, it is with all the love in my heart that I decided to write, "Twenty Years at Sea, the World as my Classroom."

Whether for a brief meeting, a day, a week, months or years and to those who I have never met, you all played a pivotal role. You have been instrumental in making me who I am and getting me to where I am today. I Love and Thank you all! It has been an incredible journey and I thank God for blessing me with such a wonderful life!

Wow...

ele

Sept 11th, 2007, 2:40 pm... I was sitting at Sam Adams Pub in JFK Airport, arriving from Athens en route to Seattle to our annual National Sales Conference. I thought it would be a sombre experience flying into New York City seven years after that unforgettable day, but everything was surprisingly normal. The bartender handed me a glass of Pinot Grigio as I waited for my order of chicken quesadillas. I took a sip of my perfectly chilled wine whilst listening to the couple next to me talking about their just-completed vacation when I realized something... I did not have a clue what day of the week it was!

If someone had told me at age 20 that I would be 50 and never married, I would have been devastated! Yet here I sit, reflecting back on my life, I shake my head and think WOW who would have imagined! I am five foot five and a half, average weight, average height, all in all – in my opinion, average. My life, on the other hand, has been far from average. I would have to rate it as extraordinary!

We all have our own personal journey through life and it is through my journey around the globe that I have found this wonderful perspective, which is truly beautiful. I have also discovered that many people are somewhat unhappy, not actually living life to the fullest, or missing some element in their life. I am so extremely grateful to have found my element and I believe that by sharing my journey, others will find theirs as well.

As I Begin my Journey ...

ele

November 4th, 1995... Five days after my phone interview, I flew to Antigua. I was greeted by a gentleman holding a sign with my name on it; he drove me to a lovely little hotel in St. John's. It was located on the waterfront in this small tourist-packed town. He informed me that he would be back in the morning to take me to the ship. I literally dropped my bags in my room and departed immediately to explore the town and try to come to terms with what was really happening in my life.

It was just before sunset as I began my walk through the narrow and uneven streets of St. John's. As I breathed in the incredible sights, joyous sounds and smells of this glorious colourful island in the Caribbean I began thinking about all that had happened to me over the past year. Truly, I was absolutely beside myself! I strolled along to the waterfront just as the sun began to set and I stared out at the spectacular sky that was bursting with colour over the peaceful sea. While taking in this precious moment of beauty and silence I realized that I was just about to turn my dream of a lifetime into reality!

Manifesting ...

~elle~

Years ago I watched the movie adaptation of Rhonda Byrne's *The Secret*. The movie featured interviews from select writers, philosophers and scientists who shared a secret - the power of intention – the law of attraction. It was at that moment that certain aspects of my life came into perspective. I am living proof, as are millions of others, that the law of attraction is true. Dreaming of what we want is a wonderful thing. However, dreaming is only the first step. If we dream about something and do nothing, we will have absolutely that – a dream and nothing more.

We can dream till we're blue in the face; until we take action it will remain a million miles away.

My father, in my opinion, was the world's biggest dreamer. He had dreams, many were multi-level marketing related, and each and every time he was about to enter into a new venture he was positive that his dreams were going to come true; mostly because he believed it had happened to others. Throughout my life, I have learned that a dream is just the start of the process. The next step is to really feel it, and honestly believe that we deserve to achieve it. However that is not all; once we have reached that point, then we *have* to take action. Taking action is a very scary step. Sometimes, it is at this point that we tend to stop, because we don't know what to do next. This is where the *real* fear sets in. Not only that, but we cannot just have one action plan; we have to have a few because guaranteed they are not all going to work. Our brain has to formulate numerous plans because if we only have one plan or idea, chances are that one idea may not work. I can still recall on numerous occasions where large quantities of various products – Amway items, personal and small home alarms, health products and essential oils – were stored all over the house for years on end; all dreams which never materialized.

When I was young, most of us, myself included, believed that in order to be successful we had to become doctors, lawyers, athletes or rock stars.

When I was younger I didn't realize that I was visualizing my dreams, I always thought I lucked into everything. However, I have personally proven time and time and time again that dreams not only *can* but also *will* come true if we really set our mind to it.

I see my life story as somewhere in between "Forrest Gump," just going with the flow and life falling into place and Wayne Dyers book "I Can See Clearly Now," a kind of jump into the stream and don't fight the current. Always have faith as life will take us where we are meant to be taken type of philosophy. As I sit here writing this book, I have absolutely no idea of what the outcome will be. What I do know is that I have an extraordinary story that I am sure many of you, for various reasons, will truly appreciate, be inspired or even empowered by to live your dreams.

Saving ...

‿ℓℓ‿

I can remember from the moment that I made my first quarter what I wanted most was to have a bank account. I have always felt the need to have some funds put away for security and let us say sanity reasons. I have never at any point in my life, ever, wanted to be rich. Nevertheless, for as long as I can remember I wanted to have some funds available so that I could do what I choose to do when I choose to do it. Early in life, I learned that if I wanted money I had to earn it. Once I began to make money as a young child my first priority was saving and I am still the same way today.

I recall during my early years of working; my friends would ask me "what are you saving for?" My response would be, "I have no idea but when I figure it out I will have the money" and I meant that statement with all my heart. I dreamed of having my own apartment fully furnished, everything brand-new and to my taste. It happened. Then a car, my first one was not brand-new but it was pretty, a white Chevy Monza with navy interior. I have always wanted everything pretty and to this day, I still do. I have been fortunate in my life; I have always had employment and have worked for a living. I realize now that was not luck, but rather that was hard work and determination.

Compelled...

~elle~

At a point in my life, I was thoroughly wrapped up in country music and Todd! He was the lead singer in a country band that played the local bars in the surrounding area. We dated for five years and even though we broke up, my love for country music stayed strong, and I appreciate him for that.

My friends and I were diehard fans at that time and on occasion would venture down to Nashville for the Annual Fan Fair Event; what a blast we would have each and every time. We would drive down and spend about a week going to different concerts. Our hope was to get a glimpse of, or up close and personal to country music's biggest stars such as Garth Brooks, Reba McEntire, George Strait & Randy Travis just to name a few. I had a dream that I desperately wanted to become a reality; it was meeting Billy Ray Cyrus. His mega-hit, *Achy Breaky Heart* was at the top of the charts and the chances of meeting him, in my opinion, were about as great as getting hit by lightning. Nevertheless, I felt compelled to try.

This statement *"I felt compelled,"* I have used numerous times throughout my life. I remember when Billy Ray was asked in an interview how he made it to the top, he humbly said, "I felt compelled to follow my dream and follow my heart," he did – it worked, and in doing so, it drastically changed his life.

I wanted nothing more at that moment in time, or in my life

for that matter, than to meet Billy Ray! Oh, my Achy Breaky Heart! I wracked my brain trying to figure out how on earth this task could be accomplished. The first part of the plan was the toughest. How do I get away from my friends? If I tell them what I am up to they are going to think that I have gone off the deep end! I knew that Billy Ray was coming to Fan Fair and that he was scheduled to be in his booth that afternoon. I told the gang that I was out for a walk, which worked. I knew that if I were to go inside, the line-up would be four hours long and that certainly was not in my game plan; I cannot stand in any line for five minutes without going snaky so I had to do something else.

I decided to go to where I thought his car was going to pull up and meet him there. I knew that even if that worked that he was not just going to open the car door and come out to greet me. I had an idea; I went to a store and bought a card. Still to this day I have no idea what the card said as that did not matter but what I do remember is that the card was in a bright red envelope. I addressed it to him, both inside and on the envelope, and signed off … *Luv Laura*. I was in position at the time I had figured he would arrive. There were a few other fans around but not many and definitely no pushing or shoving. Moreover, there I stood patiently, yet nervously waiting. I could feel in my bones that this plan was going to work.

Moments later a long white limousine came into view. The window was open and, there he was, Billy Ray. He was smiling and waving to us, his fans. I watched as the car inched towards us and it felt as if everything was literally moving in slow motion – just like in the movies. As the car pulled up, it came to a complete stop, right in front of me, and he and I were face-to-face – true story. There I stood frozen, with my arm reached out, and probably my mouth wide open. He looked at me, we made eye contact and at that moment the world stood still; he reached out and took the card from my hand, his head went into the car for a few seconds, then he reappeared and asked me "Darling what's your name?" I was in total disbelief, "OMG – Billy Ray is talking to me!" To my surprise, I could speak *and* I did remember my name. I told him, he ducked back into the car for a moment and then reappeared, reached back towards me, gave me a great big smile, returned the envelope, and as he did, he said, "Thank you, darling." On the envelope, he had written, "*to Laura, Luv Ya, Billy Ray Cyrus.*"

I felt I had accomplished the impossible and once again another dream came true! I was on cloud nine and floated back to the hotel. Upon my return, I confessed what I had done, the gang, of course, thought I was insane but I could tell, they were pleased, and I am sure a bit envious. Another lesson in my life that proves if I set my mind to something and believe it wholeheartedly, it really is possible that dreams can and do come true!

Winning ...

⌇

During my time at the bank I took part in a weekly group lottery. Bev and I were responsible for collecting the money, buying the tickets and checking the winning numbers. Everybody has hopes and dreams and the nice thing about a lottery is that by playing every week those hopes and dreams are always close by. For that reason alone, in my opinion, it is worth playing. The funny thing is that I personally never had the desire to win a lot of money, as I was always content with my life and not in need of anything substantial. My joke was and still is that my favourite brand is Wal-Mart and 50 percent off! I did, however, dream along with the rest of the group, thinking it was always nice to play in our minds "What if we do win?"

I was living with a close friend at the time. She and I had met through Mom, as they worked together at the bank. We both had split up from our exes, she moved out of her place at the same time that I had sent Todd packing. Consequently, she and I ended up being roommates – as did our exes. I casually say I sent him packing, but at the time it truly was the end of the relationship. I thought, at the time, he was the "love of my life." Although trying hard to move on, my roommate and I had an extremely tough year getting over both of these guys. We knew, however, despite the difficulties, that we were making the right decision. It was a true blessing that we met and were able to help each other through it all. My success story, which I am about to share with you, came at a rough time in my life.

I arrived home one evening, greeted my roommate and then remembered that it was Sunday. I grabbed the paper to start checking the numbers for the week. I can say I was not filled with anticipation since this was something I did weekly. Ohhh… I could not believe my eyes when the numbers started to match up – one, two, three, no way … four, five… OMG – all six winning numbers! I literally jumped up and down in my kitchen screaming, "We won – we won!" I think we all have, at least once in our lives, imagined what that moment would feel like. Talk about your stomach doing summersaults after you start breathing again that is - it was a total adrenaline rush! I ran to the corner store at the end of my street, with my heart pounding quicker than it ever had, only to realize that I had the wrong ticket in my hand – it was last week's ticket!

The good news was that we played the same numbers every week so I knew that we were still in the running. I raced back home; found the correct ticket, ran back to the store and to my total disbelief the store had closed. I looked at the locked door and all I could think was, "I need to verify this ticket, now." I went back home and we got in the car. My roommate drove because I was too excited to drive; she was too actually, but I, for sure, would have hit a tree. We drove around until we finally found a store that was open. The clerk ran the ticket through the machine and said, "I've got good news and I've got bad news. The good news is that you have all six winning numbers! The bad news is that there were five winners in total." He told us that having so many winners was highly unusual.

The following morning I went into the office and requested that my boss get the group together for a meeting but I did not tell her why. She did and once we had everyone gathered I said, "I have good news and I have bad news." I told them that we had all six winning numbers and that we had won the lottery. The group of 27 went crazy! We all worked in the second largest branch in downtown Toronto and our shrieks of joy, I am sure, could have been heard for a city block. That moment was probably the highlight of that entire experience and thinking about it today still gives me goose bumps. Okay, maybe it was one highlight, but there was more to come. Once everyone calmed down, one person said, "So what's the bad news?" I told them that we held one of five winning tickets; that there were four other winning tickets with the same numbers. The group was silent, I think everyone had stopped breathing, as they absolutely no idea what was going to be their share.

I informed them that we won approximately $7,000 each. Again the group went wild! We each had $7,000 today than we did yesterday and that was sweet. Had only our group won it, the share would have been about $34,000 each but honestly, the experience could not have been an ounce more exciting. The good news for the company was that with this amount nobody retired that day. Bev and I went to the lottery corporation to claim our prize, this too was incredibly exciting as we were filmed and interviewed by the local paper. Upon our return to work later that afternoon, as this process took quite some time, we returned to two-dozen long-stemmed red roses and a spectacular cake, decorated as a lottery ticket saying "Congratulations!" I tell you that the whole experience made me feel, honest to God as if I had won millions.

Childhood...

ele

Where do I begin with my journey? It all started with my parents as without them and their story I would not be who or where I am today. I can honestly say that I truly am one half my father and the other half my mother which makes for a very interesting personality, if I don't say so myself. My outgoingness, sharp wit and tongue are from Dad and my logical mind, level-headedness, honesty, and integrity are from Mom. One of the things I admire most about both my parents, in addition to them being great, kind-hearted and loving people, is that they have always been totally supportive of everything I have done throughout my life. They have always been there to pat me on the back for a job well done as well as to pick up all the pieces, when necessary.

My parents were born in the Netherlands. Mom was born and raised in Amsterdam and Dad in Rotterdam. They both immigrated to Canada whilst in their teens, Dad to escape from the challenges of his life and Mom to explore new horizons. They met when Mom was living with relatives in Toronto, the same relatives for who my dad came to work. Apparently, it was not love at first sight but they did fall in love shortly after getting to know each other. In 1959, eight months after they met, they were married and honoured their sacred vows "till death do us part" until Dad passed away in 2005.

They got married at City Hall and moved into a modest

basement apartment in the city. I was the first-born in January 1961 followed by my brother, John, who was born in July two years later. We lived, in my opinion, an average life in every respect. Dad was a butcher for a large grocery chain and Mom stayed at home to raise my brother and me until we were teens.

My parents were the superintendents of the four-story apartment building where we lived. My brother and I were in elementary school during those years, and as kids we were busy! We knew everyone in the building and everyone knew us. Looking back, this may be where I developed my social skills. Although in saying that, I can remember, just the thought of getting up in front of the class, even just to say my name, absolutely petrified me during my earlier years in school.

Public school was quite a walk from where we lived, about 30 minutes, which we did four times a day, as we would come home for lunch. These days, most parents would consider this unbelievable for a child to have to walk or bike that distance and would be racked with safety concerns. However, my brother and I made it through relatively unscathed while living through a few character-building incidents.

We had three route options; one of two busier streets or the winding longer scenic route which ran in between the two main streets. My brother would ride home for lunch with his friends. On this particular day, I recall being about halfway home, having taken the scenic route. As I am peddling I looked over to one of the two main busier streets where I saw a crowd gathering.

This caused my heart to skip a beat as I had sensed that something bad had happened. For a brief instant, a part of me thought to go and look, but my inner voice told me not to, and I continued on my way. Shortly after arriving home I found out that it had been my brother, who was hit by a car. All I could think was thank God I listened to my gut, as I would have been absolutely devastated seeing my brother in such a state and knowing I would have been helpless at the scene. John was six at the time; he spent two weeks in the hospital, lost a kidney, his spleen and broke his leg. The doctors said that he was quite the fighter, that he made a swift recovery and that it was a miracle that he was alive.

A few years later, I was 12 at the time; I was dog-sitting Percy an Afghan hound. He belonged to our neighbour who lived across the hall. Percy needed someone to be with him at all times or he would howl. I came home for dinner and was on my way back to mind Percy when my dad said "Be careful of the dog!" I paused and recalled thinking that to be an extremely odd statement, as I had known Percy for a few years and I loved that huge puppy, however, off I went. Moments later my parents heard a spine curdling scream and they knew instantly that it was mine.

When I had returned to the apartment, Percy was sleeping on the couch. I instinctively leaned over to greet him. I assume Percy didn't realize who it was and thought he was being attacked and without hesitation lashed out at my face. They say that you blackout, but I recall everything turning brown. Just before opening the door to flee the apartment I felt something hit the back of my leg - it was another bite from the dog. Before I realized it I was standing in the hallway of our apartment as Mom and Dad frantically ran around the apartment with horrified expressions on their faces. I have no recollection of closing the neighbour's door or opening ours. Today the memory is like that of a silent movie, hearing and interestingly feeling nothing. I recall seeing Mom retrieve a large towel, put it on my face, apply pressure and then into the van and off to the hospital we went. In a moment of crisis those affected look for their coping mechanisms. In this case, and my family still laughs about it today, Dad stopped to buy a pack of cigarettes!

I received a massive bite on my right cheek and by a miracle his jaws missed my eye, nose, mouth, and ear. Over the next three years, I underwent three plastic surgery operations to repair the damage. Approximately 150 stitches later, and I will say the doctors did an amazing job of incorporating the scar with my smile lines.

I did endure bullying; dogface was their favourite nickname for me. Despite all, I honestly don't feel that the incident or bullying affected my life or caused me any major trauma. If it was not "dogface," I would have been teased about something else. As far as being afraid of dogs – I wouldn't say that I am *afraid*; I would say that since that experience, I am cautious.

Despite being bitten I was extremely distressed about Percy's fate and the doctor noted that it would do me more harm if the dog were euthanized. Percy was spared that day. Unfortunately, it was not the last time that he attacked someone and eventually Percy was put to sleep.

Over time the scar from the edge of my smile line to my ear has faded and now you can hardly notice that there is a scar. This scar is now part of me, my facial features, and a stark reminder of how blessed I am.

Education ...

〜ℓℓ〜

When I was just about to enter seventh grade we moved to another apartment, about a mile away from where we were living. At this stage in my life, my dad was having back issues and retired from his butcher career to work for the Toronto Transit Commission (TTC) as a bus and subway driver. My mother joined the work-force and began working for the bank. This was an exciting time in my life; a new apartment and starting junior high!

In my mind, I thought we had moved to the upscale part of town. Our previous home was a modest two-bedroom, one-bathroom basement apartment. As we rode the elevator to our new home my excitement grew; we exited the elevator on the 16th floor! Not the basement, not the 6th floor, but the 16th floor – now that's movin on up! As a pre-teen, I *was* impressed.

School did not turn out to be the most memorable part of my life. I got through junior high although it was definitely *not* all that it was hyped up to be. High school was relatively normal but in my opinion, overrated. I was fortunate to have had some good friends, a few who are still friends today and acquaintances, who I still remember fondly. I can, however, still remember going through my school years feeling somewhat awkward and like an outcast around my peers.

At this point in my life, I had no idea what I wanted to have as a career. During my childhood, I wanted to be everything from a veterinarian to a flight attendant to an interior designer. Unfortunately, I sought no help in career planning while I was in school; I just figured that it would all work itself out and I just continued cruising along the road of life. I finished high school – barely. I had great grades when I was younger but they gradually fell as the years passed and like many teenagers I felt that hanging out with friends was more important and far more interesting than learning.

If you don't know what you want – any road will take you there. Lewis Carroll

So what *did* I learn from all those years in school? I do remember loving geography; however, at the time I thought what am I going to get from geography lessons other than knowing where everything is in the world. Once again I did not see how these lessons would come in handy. History was not my cup of tea, I did learn to type, thank goodness, and I attended a theatre arts class. By the completion of high school, although dealing and interacting with people was not an issue for me, getting up in front of a crowd or a camera was still a major fear! I chuckle now at my history teacher's comment to me in my last year, he said, "I wish you better luck in the workforce."

Looking back I realize that I never *loved* school; I tolerated it and made the best of the situation. It was 13 years of schedules, of being told what to do, how to do it, what to learn, how to think; being filled up with so much *stuff* that I really wasn't interested in. I just could not comprehend why on earth we needed to know all that we were being taught. Looking back, I honestly believe they should have taught things like values, self-worth, kindness, health & wellness, creativity, appreciation & gratitude. I am sure they have made great strides since I graduated almost 40 years ago but it is quite evident that we still have a very long way to go.

After graduation, we thought we were entering into the next

stage of life knowing it all; well it did not take long before I realized that the real education was just about to begin and that it would continue for an entire lifetime.

Employment ...

~ele~

I was excited, I was graduating from high school; finally, I could design my life to be everything I dreamed it to be. I decided that I was ready to go out and find me a full-time job! Growing up at the time I did, the unspoken and understood rule was, you go to school, get a job, find Mr. Right and a place to live, have kids and live happily ever after. Well, I was now at rule number two; get a full-time job. Up until this point, I had only worked part-time; first delivering newspapers, which I eventually traded in for work at the local donut shop. As far as a part-time job goes, working at the donut shop was a blast. I worked with one of my best friends at the time, we had an amazing time meeting and interacting with interesting people, plus all the free donuts we could eat!

So what does a 19-year old with only a high school diploma do? College was out of the question; I had spent all the time I was going to, sitting in a classroom. I had a close friend who worked for an insurance company - that sounded good, so I applied. Unfortunately, they did not hire me. My next step was to apply at Canadian Tire, where another friend of mine was working. I was hired as a part-time cashier. I enjoyed the work but it was only part-time so the income wasn't sufficient and deep down I knew that there had to be more to life than working as a cashier. I decided to apply for a position in the bank; it worked for my mom, so I thought I would give it a shot. I was hired as a teller and

15 years later I was still working there. Banking was an excellent career, which included numerous promotions and challenges, one of which was Assistant Manager Customer Service in Toronto's second-largest branch.

July 1991... Over a decade later, I was still employed with the bank, working for the Network Systems and Technology Support Department. I was responsible for implementing new systems (computers, banking machines etc.) and for training the staff on how to use them. I thought I was on top of the world. I was in my early 30s, had a well-paying job, working on the road travelling all over the city and outlying areas. Over the course of time, I had taken a few college and university courses offered by the bank. These courses helped bolster my position within the bank and gave me the credentials to get a number of promotions over the years. I was living on my own in my lovely little apartment back on the same street that I grew up on; I was physically in good shape, and I was financially secure. In addition to my brand new car, I had a cat, great friends, and a great family. Life was good! Along the way, I had some very interesting relationships even if always with Mr. Wrong. I truly believed that I was looking for true love, when in fact I was, unknowingly at the time, continuously looking for validation. Now, looking back, although they may not have been my Mr. Rights, and they did come with youthful heartbreaks, they also provided some very good times and very valuable lessons along the way.

With the exception of my love life, all appeared to be going well. However, despite having all my ducks aligned something was definitely missing. My ego, of course, was screaming that it was a man. My inner voice was quietly telling me that it was something else.

Weight ...

ele

It is not true what they say; man *can* live off donuts alone. Nonetheless, it would explain why I had the weight problems I did in my teen years and why Mom discreetly got me into Weight Watchers days before my 16th birthday. She was sneaky but good. I thought I was going as a favour to her but the reality was she was doing it for me, and it was a good thing she did. I lost about 25 pounds but more importantly, I learned how to eat properly and that education has helped me, despite my lifelong ongoing food challenges, forever thereafter. My initial 20-pound loss was followed by 40 years of my weight fluctuating like a roller coaster, up and down! Over the years I have put on and taken off a substantial amount of weight (probably totalling about a gazillion pounds). I would joke that I had those "size rings", like the ones used in the clothing stores to separate my wardrobe in the closet, everything from a size five to 15 – literally, depending on my weight at the time. Throughout my life, despite having gone to Weight Watchers, I have also tried every fad diet available on the market. I honestly believed at the time that each and every one of them was going to lead me to lifelong success. What I did learn from these fad diets is that you will initially lose weight; however, the pounds will sooner or later return. I have yet to meet anyone who has lost weight using an unconventional method and remained thin and healthy. In my late 20s, I went through a tougher than normal time with my weight. The fad diets weren't working and only caused me to crave bad food more than ever which led me to into a period where I suffered from bulimia. In addition to feeling bad about myself due to my increased weight, I began to withdraw from the world and would spend more and more time alone. My dating life, due to my insecurities about my self-image, went from one bad situation to another. At the time I blamed everything on earth except myself but now looking back, even I wouldn't have liked the confused and distressed me back then. All my internal drama just gave me more reason to reach for food and it escalated to the point of depression and isolation where I would secretly eat to excess and then purge. This pattern went on for almost a year and I was amazed that I was not only able to keep it to myself but I believed that the outside world looking in thought I had it all together. I did, however, realize throughout this entire time that in addition to being very dangerous, purging did not fix me, it just left me feeling very sad and very lonely. I later realized through this unfortunate time that something was lacking in my life. Fortunately, I did wake up; I finally decided that I was sick and tired of this compulsive routine and I simply stopped purging and began eating healthier foods. It wasn't long before I returned not only to my normal self but also back to the world. Shortly thereafter I got my dream job, and with joy and fulfillment in my life, I lost my desire to reach for food for comfort. To this day, however, I have to be on guard as food has had control over my life off and on throughout the years. Honestly, I will say, keeping my guard up requires a continuous conscious effort on my part. I despise the term "diet." I believe the only way to live is by developing a healthy lifestyle (which includes some type of exercise) and the interesting thing is, once we get used to it, eating healthy and being active is very pleasurable.

Signs ...

⁓

August 1992... It was a lovely summer day; I decided to go up north to my sailboat for the weekend, which was moored at a marina in Penetanguishene, Ontario. This weekend I happened to choose to go up alone, probably because of the novelty of going away every weekend with friends wore off over time. I realized that I was the one who did the planning, shopping, driving, and of course, cleaning up. I am not saying that I didn't have many glorious weekends sailing around the beautiful islands of Georgian Bay and partying up a storm with great people. However, by this time, quality alone time was also greatly appreciated, and this particular weekend was one of those times.

It was mid-afternoon, I was relaxing on deck flipping through a women's magazine; I opened to a page entitled "Women in their thirties who leave the corporate world to go work on Cruise Ships." My heart stopped! As a kid growing up watching the television show The Love Boat I had dreamed of working onboard a Cruise Ship! Up until that exact moment, I had believed that there were two things in life – dreams and reality, and I honestly did not believe that the two could be combined. I believe this is called serendipity. I did not know it at that time, but coming across that particular piece was exactly what I needed to see at that very instant in my life. My heart was racing and excitement was surging through my blood. I cut the article out of the magazine, placed it in a plastic cover and didn't put it too far away.

My only recollection of ever feeling that type of excitement was when I had vacationed onboard a Carnival Cruise when I was 23. One afternoon we were returning to the ship via one of their tender boats after a lovely day in Grand Cayman. I looked up at the vessel and for some unknown reason, at that moment viewing the ship from that angle, literally took my breath away and my heart truly felt like that once again after coming across that article.

Acapulco had become my chosen vacation spot for a few years in my 20s. I loved the mountainous backdrop that overlooked the town and the beautiful beaches; the multitude of bars and restaurants combined with dancing the night away at the clubs overlooking the bay – awesome. What more could I ask for; the weather was perfect and it was a great value for the money. Once again I encountered those unexplainable emotions, while in Acapulco for a second vacation. We were in a taxi on our way to see the cliff divers at night, as we turned a corner there she was right in front of us and all lit up, a massive cruise ship. I can remember, once again, that I gasped at the sight and my heart jumped into my throat. I knew at that moment that there was nothing more that I could want in my life than to work on a cruise ship. A vacation was not enough, I knew deep down that I wanted a cruise ship to be a part of my life. However, at that time I still viewed my emotions to be nothing more than a dream.

Another memorable moment, and possibly a sign, although it seemed like a joke at the time was while scrubbing the hull of my 25-foot sailboat. My home away from home was quaintly named "Quick Trick" by the previous owner. Mom was helping with the cleaning and I remember it as a miserably cold windy September day. I was at a point in my life that I had just about all the fun that there was to be had with my sailboat. It was becoming more of an effort than enjoyment and I was looking to sell. This feeling was not new to me; I have always been one who finds everything in life exciting until I have "been there, done that," and then I'm always looking for something "new and exciting." While diligently scrubbing, I looked up at Mom and said, "The next boat that I have is going to have a Captain!" I made that statement and I never forgot it and to this day it still makes me chuckle inside. I of course, at the time, meant a husband. I love the saying *be careful what you wish for*, as most would have never believed it – instead of a husband, I got myself a Cruise Ship!

Shortly thereafter, I was called into the office by my supervisor at the bank for my quarterly performance appraisal and to my disbelief; she said to me "I get the feeling that you are having too much fun out there." I could only imagine she was referring to when I was out on the road and in the branches training. All I could think of was, I guess I was generously using my expense account! I remember not responding. At that time in my life, despite the fact that I appeared to be very outgoing and confident – deep down, I really wasn't. I remember leaving the office thinking, *gee, if I'm having too much fun while doing my job, then I'm obviously in the wrong job!*

As it turned out, the bank was merging with a trust company and my skills were needed to assist with the merger. Not too long after that performance appraisal meeting and shortly after the completed merger, the company began downsizing and thousands of employees were offered voluntary termination packages. I looked at this offer and I had one initial thought – wow! I asked myself, how much money it would take for me to pack in my 14-year career, benefits and retirement plan. I thought about the cost of leaving the security of my job and the possible upheaval of my comfortable life, not to mention I was 32 years old. All I knew was the bank and now I would have to start over again. I was on the edge of a cliff and I needed to take a leap of faith. Accepting that offer, in my mind, at that time, was the riskiest thing I could ever do. I had been saving my entire life, did not buy anything that I could not afford and always made sure that I had some money in the bank saved for a rainy day. Up until that moment I was not really a major risk-taker, I liked the comfort, safety, and security of my life.

I decided to put in my bid to see how much they were willing to pay me to leave. I had a dollar value in my mind and when the offered amount came back it was more than I could have imagined. Oh, I thought and I thought and ... I thought some more. Can you imagine, they are willing to pay me an absurd amount of money to take the opportunity to find my real place in life? That just confirmed all that I honestly knew deep down, that my inner voice was repeatedly telling me, that I was not where I was truly meant to be. It also confirmed that I would never be truly happy; content possibly, but not truly happy, if I did not take this opportunity and find my true calling; so I did, I took that leap of faith.

Faith ...

⟋ℓℓ⟍

From the moment I had cut the article from the magazine I truly felt deep down that it was a sign. Now, I was seriously thinking about giving up my career and stability for a dream. Who does that – really? The various signs, my inner voice telling me that this is what I truly wanted, my boss's comment and the payout offer – what did all this mean? What I did know was *if I was going to do it – now was the time to take the leap!*

How on earth can I obtain something that appears to be totally out of my reach?

Where does one start? I took a deep breath and started to move forward; planning, organizing and putting my initial action plan together. The bank came to the rescue again; they were offering career counselling for anyone who had taken the package. I thought this was very considerate of them and it was exactly what I needed. I attended; it was similar to going back to school. I was certain about one thing; I had a rough few years ahead of me. Furthermore, the big question was is it going to pay off? I realized that I was not going to get an answer anytime soon. Another concern, what do I do if I do succeed? What do I do with my apartment, my car, my stuff and my cat? The questions and concerns kept coming – fears had set in and talk about feeling a sense of being overwhelmed!

In addition to taking the offered career counselling, I took a travel agent and a bartending course. I learned how to do a resume, how to network, and how to go about finding a new career. Was it easy? Not on your life, and talk about stress.

I continued to work at the bank after accepting the voluntary termination and payout, but unknown to me there was a deadline to depart, and I had passed it. I had to be not employed by the company for three months and then I could return, which I did. I came back three months later on contract working for the bank's help center. The funniest thing of all was that this position was two levels higher than my old job and I could not have possibly obtained it had I remained a full-time employee. In actuality, I had already moved up in the world without even leaving the company! I was a head office contact who assisted the branches when they had a problem that they could not resolve; then they would call me – can you imagine! In the meantime, I took my courses, worked on my resume, sent many of them out, and received not one single solitary response from anyone. I reworked my resume, sent them out again, networked, and still got absolutely no responses. I remember getting to the stage where I decided that I was going to get what I wanted or I was going to die trying. I knew that there was no in-between and at this point, there was no turning back.

September 1995... I decided that the next step of my journey was to go to the sources directly. The cruise lines head offices were all in Florida, so I convinced my friend Janice who was not working at that time to drive down with me, for moral support in finding my new career. We decided on Sept 1st as the date; we packed up the car, she picked me up from work and we were off.

Imagine the excitement, the fear and the anxiety as we set off. We decided to make an adventure out of our road trip and as we drove south we visited every one we knew between Toronto and Florida including friends of ours in New York State, my cousin in Cincinnati and Janice's mom and stepfather who were living in North Carolina. Two weeks later we arrived in Miami. We stayed with Janice's cousin and I began my search. I went knocking on doors of all the cruise lines, which once again, got me nowhere. I even got into one of the offices but the only thing I got out of that was roaming around within the office and nothing more. On the last batch of resumes I sent out I stated that I was coming down to Florida and I would welcome a meeting, I received one response from a recruiting agency in Boca Raton. I have to admit that after going to all the offices and getting absolutely nowhere I was very discouraged and ready to give up. Janice said to me, "Let's try the agency that responded." My response to her was "Yeah but it's quite a drive; it's an hour north of Miami," to which she responded, "So, we've come this far, you can't give up now!" and so we did.

I met with the gentleman who had responded, and after a very long conversation lasting about an hour and a half, he told me that I look bad on paper. Combined with the fact that I had asked for any position onboard from a cleaner to the Captain – I thought I looked keen and flexible. However, towards the end of our meeting, he told me that he felt that I had the perfect personality for a job on a cruise ship. He gave me suggestions, told me to be specific about what I wanted, asked me to update my resume and provided me with criteria for the photos required of all applicants.

We left there excited and feeling very positive about the meeting. We decided to celebrate and drive down to Key West since we were so close. It was late in the afternoon and to our complete surprise, we arrived to find the small island inundated with motorcycles – they were everywhere! We immediately realized that there was some sort of gathering and we found out a short time later that they were all in town for Fantasy Fest – Bike Week. On the famous Duval Street, every square inch was packed with thousands of bikers. The music was blaring from all the bars, people were elbow to elbow, or should I say vest to vest, with excited souls letting loose, drinking, dancing and *really* enjoying life! What amazed me most of all was the displays of body art; they were a sight to behold. It was electrifying, everyone was covered; it was a sight that many would gasp at but not me. For me, it was sheer fascination. We had a blast spending two days engulfed in the midst of this massive unique and very colourful party. We people watched and interacted with some amazing souls all the while enjoying many tasty beverages.

A few days later, we left Miami and headed north for a couple of days to visit some friends, who we had met while we were vacationing in the Bahamas the previous year. They were in Charleston on a naval ship. After an awesome two-day party with our Navy friends, the boys invited us to a retirement party for one of the officers in Norfolk. We agreed, continued to drive north and decided to stop in Myrtle Beach. We were having so much fun in Myrtle Beach that we decided to stay for an extra day; we eventually arrived in Norfolk a day later than we anticipated. We ended up having such a good time in Norfolk that we stayed there for a week and a half! Now that was a celebration USA Navy style!

We arrived home from our adventure sometime around the first or second week of October. I did as suggested regarding the resume and required photos and sent them to the recruiting agent who forwarded them along with his recommendation. On October 31st, I had a phone interview with one of the cruise lines. I don't remember the conversation but I do recall that it was Halloween, the woman on the phone asked me a few quick questions, the last being "Can you leave in four days?" – to which I responded "Of course!" Those words were followed by me holding my breath so that I wouldn't scream. At the end of the conversation I offered a sincere heartfelt thank you and then hung up the phone. I looked at my uncle, who I was living with at the time, he was standing by my side listening to my final words while obviously holding his breath as well, and then it came – the scream followed by "I did it!"

The responses from family members, friends and co-workers were really mixed. Most were very pleased that I had followed my heart and succeeded. Some, I felt were surprised that I really did make it happen and I do believe that others were sad to see me move upward and onward with my life. As for me, I was just having trouble thinking and breathing, but it was all good!

Exhilaration ...

ele

November 5th, 1995... My first thought upon awakening on that glorious sunny morning in Antigua was *is this real or am I dreaming?* Looking around the pastel-coloured Caribbean style hotel room let me know that it truly was real! I leapt out of bed, flung open the drapes, and there she was, my dream come true; the cruise ship which I now called *mine*, the beautiful *SS Meridian*. I literally jumped up and down, all by myself in the room, and screamed, "My ship is in – my ship is in!" I do not recall if I slept a wink but I do recall that I have never been so excited about anything in my entire life, including winning the lottery, and yet I was petrified at the same time.

I was in the hotel lobby at 9 am sharp, the port agent picked me up and we drove through the busy streets of downtown St. John's along the waterfront to the ship. My heart was pounding with excitement and I could not stop repeating to myself "I cannot believe that this day has come!" Before I knew it I was walking up the gangway about to enter my ship and my new life.

My heart was still pounding at the same pace when I entered the vessel. Having been on a cruise before I knew what to expect, however, now entering it as my home was a completely different story and even more exciting than my first cruise if that were possible. The Manager, in his crisp white uniform with gold and black epaulets, met us at the gangway and reached out his hand as he introduced himself. Shortly thereafter I was introduced to the team and shown to my room, I must say, although everything was very impressive, I cannot say that the happy ending occurred here.

My first contract was rough. Although being in the midst of stunning surroundings in the guest areas, the behind the scenes on this old cruise ship required getting used to for someone new to this world. My cabin was smaller than anything I could have imagined and, of course, it came with a roommate. The bathroom, however, was the best. You could do all possible duties in there, literally, at the same time. You had to make sure you used the toilet, closed the lid and put your towel outside before having a shower unless you didn't mind using either soaking wet. Imagine washing the delicates of two girls in a very small bathroom, where do we hang them? I am not sure how we managed with having to shower and our cabin only just being big enough for two bunk beds, a desk, a nightstand, and two locker room style closets. Despite these hardships, I was so extremely excited about it all; I could hardly sleep at night.

The position for which I was hired was Guest Relations Officer; I wore a bright crisp white uniform with black and gold striped epaulets now that was cool! Although I had worked with the public my whole life this was an entirely new ball game. I loved the job, but I, unfortunately, had some negative encounters with a few of the people I worked with. Let us just say they had no patience with "newbies." Structured training as we know it today did not exist and I was not a quick learner; I needed to do things a few times before I fully understood and got it right.

I survived my first Christmas and New Year's away from home as well as having left my cat, and I was missing the man who was holding my heart at the time. I had met him in Charleston and spent a week and a half with him in Norfolk. Although it was great fun while it lasted I knew before leaving that we had no future together; he was in the Navy, so ironically we were both out to sea.

We kept in touch for a while and then as ships do, we both sailed off in different directions. My cat was being well taken care of by my uncle and I learned, with regards to both, time truly does heal all wounds.

At some point in January, I ended up in tears, which lasted for days due to conflicts that I had with a couple of employees, a mini breakdown of sorts. It was unfortunate, however, and the reason I speak about it, is because I stuck it out. What stood out the most during this challenging time, was that I knew, deep down in my heart, despite the current troubles, this was exactly where I was meant to be and that this was exactly what I was meant to be doing. What I realized without a doubt was that there were just a couple of individuals who were making me feel this way and not ship life itself. I knew that it was temporary and that this challenge would pass and it did. In the meantime, I made some fabulous friends who helped me get through the hard times.

I completed my first six-month contract in May and went home for a two-month vacation. I began sharing my new experiences with everyone back home; life onboard, tales of exploring ports of call, glorious beaches, and crystal clear blue seas and it was awesome.

Returning ...

∼ere∼

My second contract was another one of my life's most memorable periods, and boarding the vessel this time around was just as exhilarating as the first time. Immediately upon arrival, the response from the crew welcoming me back was amazing. I had never in my life received such an overwhelming reception or encountered such enthusiasm and joy from others. I felt like a queen, it was unbelievable!

Although not high ranking, I was, nevertheless, an officer and I have to say that being an officer onboard a ship has its privileges. We were able to relax in the guest areas, use the guest gym, enjoy the theatre and shows and eat in the officer's mess, which in the early years came complete with white table cloths, full guest menu and our own waiters. The respect from the crew towards the officers was second nature and something I did not expect. Officers were acknowledged with a nod and always with a good morning, afternoon or evening, saying *geia sas* (hello in Greek) chief; although chief was most often used for the higher ranking male officers. Just in case I wasn't completely certain, I was now absolutely convinced that I had found the missing piece of the puzzle; I had found the place where I was truly meant to be in my life. Although that was 20 years ago, I can feel it like it was yesterday and I still cherish those feelings.

My first ship, the Meridian, as I mentioned, was an older

vessel and as it is not polite to discuss a lady's age, I will not. However, what I will say is that she, like I, had been around the block a time or two! My cabin was right at the bow of the ship down on deck three, directly above the engine room. You could literally hear each and every wave as it crashed up against the hull, which was right beside my pillow, a very interesting experience when you are trying to sleep but like anything in life, you do get used to it. One morning as I was walking down the corridor on my way to work I noticed that the floor was wet. A few steps later I saw a hole about six inches off the ground with water gushing out of it. I leaned down to put my finger in the hole. Lucky for me someone else had come out of his cabin at that moment and he went to get help. I remained there, waited patiently for help to arrive, feeling like the little Dutch kid in the story, who saved Holland by putting his finger in the dike. It turned out that on the other side of the wall was the men's shower. The drain was clogged and the water backed up into the stall and was making its way out into the corridor. I may not have saved the ship from sinking that day but I'm sure the carpenters appreciated me saving them the work of replacing the carpet.

This contract was amazing; I had learned to perform the necessary duties and with each passing day became more efficient thus earning the respect of those around me, which of course was the best part. I met some incredible people, some became lifelong friends, the closest being my roommate Barbara. She was 19 years old and from Montreal, a beautiful girl inside and out. It was her first contract and she and I instantly became best friends. During our off time, we enjoyed shopping, tasting new foods and sight-seeing. We were fortunate and enjoyed the beaches and islands of the Caribbean in the winter months and the pink sand beaches of Bermuda during the summer. That and, of course, we partied our asses off. Funny, I realized why when you first get on a cruise ship you can't or you're afraid to go to sleep – for fear of missing out on some of the fun. One of the biggest challenges, next to dealing with the public, was being at work on time and appearing to be sober! Ah yes – but those were the good old days!

Those of us working at the guest relations desk were responsible for making public and safety announcements onboard the ship. Announcements ranged from final requests for local visitors onboard to return to shore prior to the ship leaving port, to events around the ship, such trap shooting, aka skeet shooting. For environmental reasons, trap shooting was short-lived on cruise ships. At first, I was petrified when I had to make an announcement but again, with anything we *have* to do, once we do it enough, fear dissipates and we get better at it with time – usually! One afternoon it was my turn to make the announcement. I took a deep breath and held down the red button, listened for the three-toned bongs which rang out over the ship's loudspeakers. I paused and then said, "Good afternoon ladies and gentlemen, may I have your attention, please. We would like to advise our guests that in 15 minutes' time we will begin *twapsooting* out on deck six aft" (aka- rear of the ship). I froze, but it was too late, it was done, announced to the entire ship! Moments later, the phone rang, I answered, it was the Cruise Director; he said "Twapsooting!" Although extremely embarrassing at that moment, I will say we all had a good laugh over that one for quite some time. Of course, that wasn't the only incorrect announcement made, it happened on occasion, people reporting the wrong gangway location, incorrect shore excursion meeting place or even the wrong port of call that we were in or were on our way to – now that's always fun.

It was the middle of the afternoon and I was working with Barbara. We had a special needs group onboard for the cruise. On deck five there was a guest elevator in the middle of the lobby and in that elevator was a joyriding guest who eluded his caregiver. It so happened that the elevator was directly across from the Guest Relations Desk where we were stationed. Every time the door would open he would give us all a great big full toothy smile and wave. We weren't quite sure what we should do. I suggested to Barbara, "Let me try; maybe I can help get him to where he wants to go." I entered the elevator and he immediately grabbed my hand, looked up at me and gave me another great big beautiful smile, and then held my hand tight. He had absolutely no desire to go anywhere. He was having a great time doing what he was doing and would make a fuss if I even tried to assist him out of the elevator. Therefore, for the next 20 minutes, we rode the elevator. Every time Barbara heard the elevator chime she looked up, we exchanged a type of knowing glance combined with our ear-to-ear smiles. This was a shared experience of love and nurturing. We both chuckled of course until his caregiver came by the desk to report him missing and thus helped relieve me of my "duties." These are just a few cherished moments onboard!

Romance ...

∾ℓℓ∾

August 1996... Whilst at home during my first vacation, I remember thinking; I would really love to meet someone and have a serious relationship. It was shortly after that contemplation when I arrived on board and a young good-looking Greek Apprentice Engineer caught my attention. I would see him periodically in the corridors and in the Officer's mess; we always made eye contact and he would smile at me. That beautiful smile of his and his "*Hallo*" in his charming Greek accent always made my day.

As opportunity would have it, he and his friends appeared at a party my new roomie and I were having in our cabin. Remember, I really only saw him in passing, but the electricity was there and now I got to see him in a relaxed environment, unwinding and enjoying himself. He became more enticing!

During an overnight stay, while docked at the Royal Dockyard in Bermuda, my friends and I went out for dinner and then to the local disco, both located within walking distance of the ship. I was standing alongside the dance floor with a good friend, just observing the crowd when I spotted *him* on the dance floor. It was then and there I nudged my friend to look over at my young engineer and said, "I want that man!" Was it the drinks I had consumed throughout the evening? Was it the music? At that exact moment, the music magically changed to a slow song. Without pausing, I walked over and asked him to dance. After three glorious slow dances, the music suddenly changed; it was loud, fast, and the entire place lit up with the bright flashing colourful lights. He looked into my eyes and said, "Would you like to go for a walk," to which I immediately responded, "I would love to." Giannis and I strolled through the grounds of the dockyard, surrounded by the fortresses and majestic old buildings, which were being lit by the landscape lighting. The warm night breeze, the stars and the moon combined with the illuminated cruise ship lights made the night all that more inviting. He then looked over at me, slowly slipped his arm around my waist and pulled me close. We looked into each other's eyes for what seemed to be a very long moment and then we kissed; after which I floated back to the ship, the two of us arm in arm. I can remember him kissing me goodnight at my cabin door and then he left. Once inside my cabin, I threw myself on my bed and realized I was smiling from ear to ear. I did pinch myself to make sure that this night and everything that happened in it was in fact real! Three slow songs later, a walk, a kiss and it is as if only he and I existed. The following evening Giannis returned to visit and became my roommate for the rest of the contract, and that is ship life!

Life with him was always an adventure. It was customary to have Greek themed nights for the predominately Greek Officers onboard. They were hosted for various reasons such as their "Name Days," and birthdays, but "Greek Easter" was the best; long tables with white tablecloths and bottles of wine, always a large array of specialties which included roasted lamb on a spit, grilled pork, lemon chicken and potatoes, Greek salad, baklava and much more. The Greek music would be blaring and between the food, music, dancing and all of the Greek conversations, you felt as if you were a part of a large Greek family gathering. They would even go so far as to bring out the plates for their official plate smashing ceremony, however that custom ceased a few years later, in Greece as well. It was replaced, for safety, cost and clean up reasons, with carnations; onboard, we would use paper napkins. At some point, a song would come on and the guys would always jump up out of their chairs and sing along while expressing their emotions with dramatic hand motions, it was automatic as if they just could not resist.

It was on one of these nights that Giannis took center stage; his arms stretched out and his head proudly held high, with the other Officers behind him, all down on one knee, slowly clapping to the music. He spectacularly performed a dazzling Greek Dance. I was in awe. At that moment, without him even knowing it, he reached out and grabbed my heart and my heart never looked back.

We remained a couple for the duration of that contract, getting along very well and loving our time together. As an engineer, he rotated between working and going to school and it was time for him to return to school. He was scheduled to leave the vessel two months before I finished my contract and he would not be back to ships for the remainder of the year. Onboard relationships happen; a phrase was even coined, "till the end of contract do us part," and accordingly I began to wonder if his leaving was going to be the end of our relationship.

Totally to my surprise, just before he left, he invited me to visit him in Greece. Although I was thrilled at the offer I instantly became concerned; there was a marked age difference. I was not sure if his family was going to accept his 12.5-year older woman.

I offered to go in the guise of a "friend." However, knowing how we felt about each other and age not being a factor in our relationship he decided, in the end, to be honest with his family before my arrival. I can't say that his mom was pleased; was it the age difference or was the major concern me not being Greek *and* in her opinion too old to have children? Although we had agreed that we would see each other again in the near future, parting ways was very difficult and left me very sad.

Vacation came three months later and I was off to see Giannis.

I flew from Toronto to Athens and would be catching a connecting flight from Athens to Thessaloniki. Just as I joined a very long line they announced last call for the boarding of my flight. I stood there, my heart stopped as I looked at what felt like 100 people ahead of me. Out of sheer fear that the people would kill me for cutting the line, I dropped my bag in the middle of the airport, and ran to the front of the line, interrupted the check-in clerk and told her of my situation. She politely asked me if I had a bag to check-in, I said, "Yes," and pointed to the middle of the departure hall. She saw that I was still in a panicked state and calmly told me to retrieve my luggage and she would check me in! I think my heart started to beat normally again about 30 minutes later, just in time for the descent, only to have the anxiety ascend, pushed by the excitement and apprehension of seeing Giannis.

I disembarked the plane, it was a very cold 12 degrees Celsius, and I could feel my heart pounding as I approached the terminal. Just as I walked inside, I felt someone come up beside me and gently tug on my ear. I swung around; there stood Giannis with his arms open wide and with the cutest grin from ear to ear. I threw myself into his arms and at that moment, all that we had gone through, and every painful second we were apart over the past few months was worth it. We retrieved the luggage and got into the car. I knew then that Giannis was just as nervous and excited as I was as he put the car in gear, backed up in error, into the fence behind us! No damage to the car, only to his pride, we both chuckled and off we went. He had arranged for us to spend a night at a hotel to reunite before going to meet his best friends in Thessaloniki and then it was home to meet the family.

Meeting his mom, to my surprise, went very well. Her favourite story she would retell was when he and I walked into the house for the first time. He entered through a very narrow hallway from the kitchen to the living room, with me tucked right behind him. His mother could not see me; she asked him jokingly if I didn't show. Later on, as she retells the story, she noted that it was because I was tiny and I was hidden behind her tall son. During my three-week stay her preconceived notions of me and her vision of not liking me were dispelled. Although she was still concerned about the age difference and the children issue, she did grow to love me.

My time spent with Giannis in Greece was marvellous. We travelled to the countryside and spent glorious evenings at the nearby tavernas enjoying the local food and wine or just relaxing at home. When the time came to part ways once again, Giannis didn't want me to go and asked me if I would consider staying. We both knew that it might be a year before we would have the opportunity to be and work together once again. Despite my heart screaming "Stay," I said I could not. I had many reasons; debts, my desire to work and travel the world, to loving my life onboard. Regardless of my decision, I could not have imagined how painful our upcoming farewell would be.

Upon arrival at the check-in counter, the agent said that there were seats available and asked if I would like to catch an earlier flight to Athens. We simultaneously said "No!" as we did not want to lose a single moment. We quietly sat watching the planes, saying very little, just drinking in our few remaining moments together. The goodbye was excruciating. I crossed the tarmac and when I was just about to set foot up onto the stairs leading to the plane, I stepped back, leaned around the nose of the plane to see if I could see Giannis one last time, but I did not. He told me later that he was there, that he watched me disappear and then reappear. He said that his heart stopped as he honestly thought at that moment that I had changed my mind. He told me about the woman standing by his side, him in tears; she must have been wondering what on earth! He said he did not care and I too spent the first half of that flight in tears once again, due to a broken heart.

I returned to the ship. While walking along the beautiful

pink sands of Bermuda admiring the glorious sea with its various tones of blues and turquoise, the water so clear revealing rocks, sand and vibrantly coloured fishes below the surface, it was then I knew I was blessed. However grateful for that feeling I also felt extreme loneliness. Travelling the world is truly one of life's greatest blessings but having the opportunity to do so with someone you love makes it perfect. Shortly after our departure, Giannis and I decided that neither of us could wait until the following year to reunite. He came to Canada for three weeks during his Christmas break allowing us to spend the holidays together and to meet my entire family. They absolutely adored him and it was another amazing vacation. I returned to work in January and Giannis went back to school. The following July I returned to Greece for another awesome romantic summer vacation. It was not until October that I returned to work.

Drama ...

∽

Three years into my cruise ship career and beginning my fourth contract I was once again faced with a personal challenge. At the end of my previous contract, I put in a request to be on the same ship as Giannis and it was approved. However, due to staffing shortages, I was transferred to another ship. I was told that this would be a temporary assignment and that I would be transferred back to *"our"* ship as soon as was possible. In my cruise ship career thus far I was fortunate to work with incredible shipmates; however, this contract, that was not the case.

This was a fascinating team of girls. They gave competition a new definition by going out of their way, bending over backwards in order to outshine each other, even if it meant putting others down. They pointed fingers and were famous for saying one thing and then doing something else. The backstabbing was like nothing I had ever experienced in all my years of working, the bank included. Despite this much less than perfect situation, I did realize that once again, the situation was temporary and reminded myself that this too would pass.

As Christmas approached I decided that dealing with this situation would be best solved by volunteering for the midnight shift – for a month, allowing me to have little contact with the team. In addition, Christmas music was no longer piped throughout the ship – a politically correct move and I was away from

Giannis during the holidays. My midnight request was granted; I got to enjoy the peacefulness of being away from the team and have my days off to explore the ports of call. I was also able to enjoy my Christmas music without offending anyone.

Sometimes what may seem as just playful fun to you may not be that for others and can jeopardize your career. As I was heading to my cabin after my shift, I heard the girls laughing hysterically and I had to poke my head into Jill's cabin to find out why. They were all dressed in nurse scrubs. It was the last night of the cruise and they were all planning to go to the staff bar and invited me to join them. I told them that if I had a set of scrubs I would and moments later they were handed to me. It was hilarious – the *official three* nurses and the *three of us*, six in total parading down the crew corridor – affectionately referred to onboard as the 1-95. As we paraded by the crewmembers, they would turn in disbelief when not one, two or three nurses walked by but four, then five and then six; everyone was laughing hysterically especially all of us. We were in the staff bar, enjoying ourselves, having drinks, letting off steam when the door opened and the senior doctor looked in, and by the look on his face he was not impressed.

The following morning we all were summoned to the Staff Captain's office where we received written warnings. It could have been a lot worse as the violation was for imitating medical personnel, which is a cause for dismissal. We apologized and signed our warnings, which meant that we had to be on our best behaviour for a while.

Despite that small disciplinary incident, my transfer was not jeopardized. I would be with Giannis once again.

Caribbean ...

⌒ℓℓ⌒

The taxi I was in turned onto a small road in San Juan, as it made a right turn towards the pier, I looked up and there she was. I gasped – she was beautiful and huge! I had heard horror stories about working on this particular ship, that it was jinxed and that anything that could go wrong did. I did not care. I was going to be back with my man and I was ecstatic. My reunion with Giannis was just as exciting as that moment at the airport in Greece when I felt him tugging on my ear. My team was made up of an old room-mate and friends I had previously worked with. It was a trifecta; I was back in the beautiful Caribbean while those back at home were enduring cold and snow – life was perfect!

A saying shared by crewmembers is "We were all there for a good time, not a long time," because people were always coming and going. However, during my life as a traveller, there is one thing that is constant, and that is the beauty of our surroundings.

It was a February evening and standard departure time was 6 pm; I had worked the morning shift so I decided to go out on deck to watch our departure and the last moments of total daylight. The sunset and combined sail away from the port of Charlotte Amalie provided an incredible view of the town nestled into the surrounding mountains; decorated with colourful houses like ornaments on a Christmas tree. Directly to the right of the vessel were shops and about 0.5 mile to the left was the downtown core.

The view from the bow was of shops, restaurants, condominiums and the marina with a variety of yachts, some so large that they housed "toys," everything from jet skis, to smaller boats to helicopters. Leaving St. Thomas was always a breathtaking event. Once away from the pier this big gal would manoeuvre through all the small inlets and coves, inches away from tiny boats while gliding through the crystal clear blue water. The scenery changed minute by minute and each and every view was spectacular whilst combined with a breathtaking sunset. Just about 45 minutes after our departure the sun would give us one last fleeting glimpse of this darkening island; leaving us the silhouette of the mountains dotted by thousands of tiny lights coming from downtown and the outlying areas. It truly was the way to relax; watching the island slowly become smaller in the blacking distance while listening to the rush of waves from the wake off the stern. This was one of the most peaceful times to sit out on the back deck.

Caribbean cruises often appeal to first time cruisers for many reasons. Most are seven nights in duration, cost-effective and flights from North America are less expensive than flights to other destinations in the world. This is also why a Caribbean cruise attracts a younger crowd and families allowing them to escape the cold winters, bathe in the sunshine and lounge on beautiful beaches while enjoying reggae music and beverages in coconuts with umbrellas.

If you prefer not to play on the beach you can explore the sea; swim with dolphins, turtles, stingrays and sharks as well as snorkelling, possibly exploring reefs and shipwrecks. Activities abound for the adventurer in us; sailing, kayaking, jet skiing, parasailing, and windsurfing. Once you tire of the sea, you can explore the spectacular nature of the islands, historic fortresses, and numerous caves. How could I not mention the abundance of duty-free diamonds, emeralds, liquor and a variety of merchandise; a gift for everyone!

My favourite *must-see* destination in the Caribbean is the Pitons on the island of St. Lucia. This excursion takes guests across this beautiful lush island, through the rainforest, stopping at a local fishing village. You then arrive at the Pitons, a famous landmark of two twin volcanic spirals soaring out of the sea for an awe-inspiring view and photo opportunity followed by a local lunch. After lunch, you can enjoy snorkelling off a black sand beach located in a little cove surrounded by black volcanic rocks in the midst of a tropical rainforest. Your return to the ship is sailing onboard a catamaran while enjoying tropical beverages. In my humble opinion, life in the Caribbean does not get any better than that!

Alaska ...

ele

At the beginning of April, I headed home for a few weeks of vacation and returned to my ship in May, which was docked in Vancouver. Shortly after arriving on board, as I was getting ready for my first shift my manager called; our sister ship that was docked across from us on the same pier needed assistance. They were short-staffed and needed someone to fill in for two weeks on their upcoming two cruises. Giannis and I discussed it – it was only for two weeks, so another kiss good-bye and off I went. The aggravation of getting from one ship to another and having to deal with customs, immigration *and* security *again* was going to be a nightmare.

Despite having to leave Giannis and my friends, this stint would be a different Alaskan itinerary, something I looked forward to doing. The ship was scheduled for a 7-night northbound cruise from Vancouver to Seward and then a return 7-night southbound cruise from Seward to Vancouver. This route added a few new ports of call and cruised a little further north than my ship's 7-night round-trip from Vancouver itinerary. It also gave me the opportunity to meet some new people and to reunite with some I had not seen for a while.

After finishing my shift I went to the guest gym to workout. The gym was located at the front of the ship on deck 10 above the bridge and spanned from one side of the ship to the other – a panoramic 180-degree view. I can remember gasping as I turned the corner when entering the gym. It was one of the most, if not *the* most spectacular sight that I had ever seen at that point in my travels. It was early in the evening; the sun was setting and directly ahead of the ship was the face of a gigantic wall of snow. It stretched up all the way to the snow-capped peaks atop the mountains as far as the eye could see in either direction. It was as if we were about to sail right into them, we were so close that I had to walk right up to the windows and look up to see the peaks. I did not recall up until that moment in my life seeing such a sight so vast and so incredibly beautiful. A photo could not have possibly captured it all; it was once again, another Wow moment in my life!

As agreed upon, I assisted for the two cruises and then returned to my originally scheduled ship and my Giannis to complete my contract.

These cruises were designed to showcase Alaska's beauty and wildlife. We sailed up the coast of Vancouver between Victoria and the mainland. We then sailed to Ketchikan, Skagway and Juneau where we docked for sightseeing. Ketchikan offers an awesome wildlife cruise to Alaska state park that allowed us to get a view of many different kinds of wildlife including bald eagles, Dall's porpoises, seals and whales. Once again, in my opinion, the whales stole the show! I had the opportunity to go out on a zodiac or cruiser a few times over the years and although it's never guaranteed, I had the chance to get up close and personal with these gentle giants every time. It was as if they were waiting for the smaller boats with tourists to come out so that they could proudly show their majestic beauty for all to admire. It truly is an experience of a lifetime!

As with my first experience in the guest gym, this cruise also offered a breathtaking view of the Alaskan Glaciers. In past cruises that I served on, we went to Glacier Bay and in the later years, we would visit Hubbard Glacier. Both were awe-inspiringly spectacular sites. Nothing compares to standing what felt like an arm's length away from these massive, turquoise and white walls of ice. I pass no judgement! I cannot say that one was better than the other. If the sight of these imposing walls of ice was not breathtaking enough, the experience of being right there when they calve is unbelievable; birthing huge chunks of ice that break off glaciers falling into the icy waters. With a thunderous crash echoing through this serene environment this is one of life's treasures not to be missed.

Alaska offers up some wonderful surprises; shortly after waking one morning, I opened the drapes and through my porthole, I saw a clear day with very calm seas. Fifteen minutes later as I was stepping out of the bathroom, I turned to the porthole and witnessed a site. The porthole had framed the tail of an Orca whale as it made its descent into the ocean. It was there just long enough for me to capture a snapshot in my mind before it descended back into the water. Now that is definitely the perfect way to begin your day.

The *Hanger* and the *Twisted Fish* are two of my favourite reasons to have the night off in Juneau. Crab legs, shrimp and portobello mushrooms, it didn't matter; either was equally as good in both food quality and ambiance. Juneau also gave me the opportunity to take flight excursions over the glaciers. One of these excursions included an expedition to Mendenhall Glacier, where we went glacier trekking. We were outfitted in full gear, including special spiked ski boots (crampons), ice axes, rows, suspender belts, and helmets. As treacherous as the terrain was it was also an exhilarating experience.

One of the best-kept secrets of this particular cruise is the breathtaking scenic sail away from Skagway in the evenings. On deck 12 the view off the bow as the ship sailed at dusk through the narrow passageway between the snow-capped mountains and the Alaskan wilderness was mesmerizing. There would only be a handful of people around which contributed to the stillness of the evening. Regardless of the weather, especially with fog or mist, the viewing was always different, would never disappoint, and never got old. Those particular sailings are one of my definitions of peace on earth.

Reminiscing ...

A mixture of the awe-inspiring Alaska wilderness and long comfortable, wine-infused conversations with Barbara took me back to reminiscing about experiences from my past, which were also pivotal moments in my life.

Summer 1973... I, as most kids did, went to summer camp by bus or our parents drove us; summer camp was usually a few hours' drive from home. However, my summer camp of 1973 was decidedly different. My parents were sending me to the Netherlands to visit my grandparents for the summer. This was an opportunity to get to know my relatives and learn a little bit of Dutch. As a bonus to my European vacation, I got to spend a few weeks in the port city of Malaga, Spain, on the coast of the Mediterranean Sea. My aunt and uncle had a home in the coastal mountains outside of the city. As exciting as this vacation seemed, as an awkward 12-year old combined with a language barrier, I was less than excited by the entire experience. What did come out of this childhood adventure was that I developed the desire to travel and see the world; this may have been the spark. Who knows?

Summer 1984... In my early 20s, I decided to return to Europe for a year-long holiday. In order to fulfill this dream vacation, I would have to quit my job at the bank. As it was, I was also in the honeymoon stage of my relationship with Todd – a nice complication in my life! For a brief moment, I contemplated cancelling my year-long trip altogether. Since 61 days of my trip were booked on the Contiki Grand European Tour, I chose to go to Europe for four months, instead. I was not granted the time off work, and I did have to quit my job at the bank. In May I departed for my four-month adventure.

My first stop was the Netherlands where I spent time with my relatives. It was a fantastic visit this time around, a much better memory than when I was 12 years old. After my two-week stay, I was off to London to begin the 61 days of touring Europe. I arrived at Amsterdam airport just in time to miss my flight; I had misread the ticket. I read the arrival time in London as the departure time! A few hours and many dollars later – the cost of being careless, I was off to London.

The Contiki Grand European Tour was a two-month organized "casual" bus tour with almost 50 Australians. We stayed in Contiki villages that consisted of tents and cots and were pre-set-up at every stop. In addition to the regular Contiki stops, we had many special stops with accommodations such as chateaus, chalets, castles and even small huts. The staff at each stop organized the set-up and the food; we did assist in minor prepping and clean up. Other than that the only thing we had to worry about was getting on the bus on time for departure the following morning.

Looking back at the photos 30 plus years later, I have minimal recollection of any of the 31 spectacular cities that we visited, as it appears that we partied all night and slept all day on the bus!

At the completion of our 61-day tour of 14 countries which included France, Spain, Italy, Greece, Turkey, Yugoslavia (at that time), Germany, Austria, Switzerland just to name a few, I decided to travel up to Northern Europe. I travelled to Stockholm, Sweden; Copenhagen, Denmark; Helsinki, Finland; and to Oslo and Bergen in Norway by train with my new friend Carla from Australia who I had met on the bus tour.

There were no beds available in the hostels on the night we arrived in Copenhagen. I went from having everything completely organized for me to have to spend the night sleeping on a train station bench. It was not nearly as much fun; I had become a spoiled princess. It was, however, another very interesting adventure in another spectacular part of the world.

I returned to Toronto and inquired about getting my job back and I did. My relationship with Todd continued for about a year down a rocky road, which led us to eventually parting ways. Carla and I remained friends; the following year she did a US Contiki tour and included a trip to Canada to visit me for a few weeks.

Two years later I flew to Townsend, near Cairns, Australia, for a two-week Contiki "party our butts off" tour. This tour took us to Brisbane, the Sunshine Coast and Sydney. I then flew to Melbourne to spend a delightfully relaxing week with Carla. The trip was a blur; in addition to it being a two-week party.

What I do recall to this day was my overnight stay in Sydney as I waited for my return flight home. I had a very early flight so I was up and out of the hotel just as the sun was rising. The hotel was at the top of a hill. As I opened the door and stepped outside I took a deep breath of the morning air. As I turned to the right to begin my descent down the street I was greeted by the silhouette of the Sydney Harbour Bridge and the Opera House; they were awash in a brilliant array of colours; yellow, orange, shades of red and violet all from the rising sun in the background. It was an unbelievable moment, and I chuckled as the strangest thought entered my mind. Here I was halfway across the world, a million miles away from home, and staring at this miraculous view, when I realized at that exact moment that I only had $35 in my pocket. I said to myself, life really is – truly amazing!

Millennium ...

⟳

December 1999... Throughout my life, I had a vision of being at sea celebrating or participating in the millennium celebration, even before working on a cruise ship. I was now five years into my career when I was asked to step up as Guest Relations Manager. This was a very big deal on two levels; I would be in charge of a major celebration - the Millennium Holiday sailing and I would be in charge of the team. This offer came six weeks prior to my scheduled vacation. Any sane soul would have said, I am flattered, but no thank you and then go home to enjoy the holidays. Not me, I had been waiting for this moment! As I received and accepted this offer, Giannis, who was finishing his contract onboard, was told he would be on another ship for his next assignment.

Sadly, as much as we loved each other, Giannis and I decided to part after his contract ended. Prior to my position as a Guest Relations Manager, I was able to request transfers to be with him. However, the new position did not allow that flexibility. I also chose to stay with this particular ship – she was sailing to Europe in a few months – which would be another dream come true.

We spent our farewell evening out in San Francisco. In my photos, we look like two sad puppies. Although it was excruciatingly painful to say goodbye again, this time possibly for good, deep down I knew that I was doing the right thing.

After a brief handover, I began as Guest Relations Manager

on December 12th. With that came the realization that Christmas was right around the corner. With Giannis gone I was not at all in the spirit of things, which was sad, because I am usually the one who is all pumped for Christmas. Despite my feelings, I had a responsibility to keep the spirits high for my staff of 10 who were a world away from their families.

Holiday Cruises are known to be the most challenging due to many factors. The ships are fully booked; guest expectations are greater, unpredictable weather, flight challenges causing guests to miss the ship and a lot of lost luggage with Christmas gifts. There are also many guests who cruise to get away from the holidays and don't want to see it onboard either which leads to the guest concerns of too much or too little of the holiday spirit around the vessel.

I ventured on to the island of St. Thomas, with no plans or expectations. As I was out walking around the town, thinking about my new responsibilities and feeling the Christmas blues, my inner voice said: "It's time to pull your socks up and get with the program!" I purchased Christmas decorations, presents for all of my employees, wrapping paper and all the trinkets to go with it. I realized how the Grinch felt when he decided to give Christmas back to Whoville – my heart was bursting with joy! What came over me next was truly amazing. I returned to the ship laden with bags and totally rejuvenated and ready to make this holiday season the best ever for all. The entire staff was in the holiday spirit; they decorated the offices, a gift exchange was organized for Christmas Eve and we had a fabulous Christmas dinner with all on Christmas day in the officer's mess.

A few days after the holidays we had our scheduled team meeting. As I stood facing the group, just about to address them, one of my team members stepped forward and said, "We have something for you." I was taken aback. They presented me with a card and a beautifully wrapped gift; my immediate thought was that this gift was far too pretty to open. When I opened and read the card I could have cried. They all thanked me for making their holidays away from home special. They each thanked me for giving them the best Christmas at sea. The accolades were heartfelt and beautiful. Eventually, I did have to open my gift. The content was beyond belief; a beautiful Mont Blanc Pen, it was black and gold. To this day, as I pick up that pen, I am brought back to that day, where I was filled with a sense of pride and love.

Our Millennium Holiday Cruise, although challenging as hell, went very well; my team was happy, they did a great job and I survived the heartbreak of Giannis and I parting ways. They say the best way to get over the pain is to keep busy and with this new position – that I did.

I believe that I rocked as Guest Relations Manager in every aspect and left that contract feeling good about my accomplishments and more importantly good about myself.

Principle ...

～ele～

Although I loved working at Guest Relations, I decided that it was time for me to take on new challenges and to increase my income. Prior to my accepting the temporary relief position of Guest Relations Manager, I had requested to be Group and Sales Coordinator. My request was granted and I was ready for the next step in my career, but at what price, my principles?

April 2000... I was informed by a fellow crewmember who was leaving for vacation that while at the Crew Pursers desk she spotted an airline ticket with my name on it. Unfortunately, this method of short notice transfer was common practice in the industry. That could only mean one thing; I would be departing at the next port, which was Barbados, in a few days' time. I heard the jokes and rumours; another Group and Sales Coordinator of Greek descent whose son was joining our ship as a Purser was granted a transfer to be with him and sail to Europe. I had taken it as a joke. I had been with the company for a little over five years, doing a great job and could see no reason why this would happen.

Well, it turned out, it did. The office claimed that it was due to the high volume of foreign-speaking guests and that I did not speak any other languages. I reviewed the projected forecast of foreign guests and they were minimal compared to what I had dealt with in the past. What on earth do you do when such injustice is about to happen?

As the Captain passed my office I took the opportunity to pose this question to him, "What could the company do if I refused to leave?" He told me – worst-case scenario, they could tell you that they no longer require your services and let you go, paying you for the rest of your contract. That would be about three-months pay. I thought about it briefly and decided that I was going to stand up for not only my rights but for all the crewmembers who could not afford to stand up for themselves.

I garnered the names of the top six executives in the company from the president down and I sat down at my pc and wrote a letter. I expressed my concerns about not only my circumstance but also that of other crewmembers who cannot or choose not to voice their concerns on short notice transfers. After re-reading the letter a few times, I took a deep breath, hit enter and went to bed.

The following morning I could see by the return receipts that all of the recipients had received it. I took another deep breath and continued with my day. A few hours later I received a call from HR shore side. As a response to my email, she agreed that the reasoning behind the staffing change was unjust; however, unfortunately, it was done and at this point could not be reversed. She asked me if I would agree to a transfer to another ship. I said that I would not, as in my mind doing so would mean that I was consenting to what had happened. I informed them that if this decision was not reversed that I would be going home.

As I waited for a response from HR, my replacement came on board. I had requested one week to prepare myself professionally and personally – to put my affairs in order.

One week later, with no word from the office, I was on my way home. The support that surrounded me both onboard and ashore was astonishing. Giannis and I had been in contact during these times and he too was very supportive of my decision to stand up for myself. However, at that point, I realized that I had lost this battle. Despite the loss and feeling devastated over what had happened, I was so proud of myself for standing up for what I believed in. Another major wow moment in my life!

I knew deep down that I really did not want to give up a career that I truly loved and in my mind, I had decided what *I* wanted. I wanted to transfer to the vessel that Giannis was on, as a Guest Relations Officer at my current salary until my current position became available once again.

Shortly after my departure, the office had emailed the ship with a few offers – I could transfer to the other ship as originally scheduled by the office, take compassionate leave or I could transfer to Giannis' ship as Guest Relations Officer. Unfortunately, I had already left for home prior to the ship receiving confirmation of these offers.

Five days after arriving home I received a phone call from head office. There were now two positions available on Giannis' vessel and I could catch the ship in five or seven days. I asked, "At my current salary?" The response was that unfortunately as I did not finish my contract and left the ship, I had therefore officially resigned. This meant that I would now be starting a new contract. In my mind this battle was not finished; it was a matter of principle. I responded that I would not take a decrease in pay and would only return at my current salary. I was placed on hold for 20 minutes; she came back and agreed to my terms.

I did not share this experience to boast that I won a battle. Rather I wanted to share how standing up for your values and what you believe in is a win all around. I followed my heart. I knew that I had to stand up for myself and face the challenges before me and in doing so it not only strengthened my character but also altered my future dramatically – for the better.

Grateful ...

May 2001... I flew to Vancouver to meet the ship; we were cruising Alaska for the summer. Upon my return I was greeted by crewmembers I knew, as well as Giannis. We picked up where we left off; it was as if we never parted.

In June I was asked if I would be willing to assist on another ship for two months as Group and Sales Coordinator. I saw this as a great career opportunity; however, Giannis wasn't pleased that we would be separated once again. I agreed to do it providing they would allow me to return after the two months of service. Another request I made was that upon completion of this two-month Alaska contract I was to return for three weeks to spend time with Giannis and my parents who were taking this Alaska cruise. I finished my contract on August 31st. Both ships were docked in Vancouver; I transferred over as a visitor, my parents arrived and we were all aboard to begin our 14-night Alaskan vacation.

Devastation ...

~ele~

People were jumping from the higher floors of the towers and then, if all of that wasn't totally beyond comprehension, I watched in absolute horror as the south tower crumbled before our eyes into a cloud of dust. Two hours after the first impact, both towers had collapsed and were gone; New York City was engulfed in a massive cloud of dust.

September 11th, 2001... The ship arrived in Sitka early that morning; the phone rang shortly before 8 am waking us both. Giannis answered the phone; it was Mom, who said, "Turn on the TV!" We tuned in to see that a plane had flown into the north tower of the World Trade Center. I immediately thought it was an accident until they aired the second plane striking the south tower approximately 20 minutes later. At that moment we knew that it definitely was not an accident. I was not able to pull myself away and remained glued to the TV, watching as a third plane hit the Pentagon and the fourth plane crashing in a field in Shanksville, Pennsylvania.

Later on in the day Mom called again and asked me if we should go out, as we may never have this opportunity to see Sitka again. We did go ashore by tender boat. It was the eeriest feeling walking through this beautiful little Russian-style town with its approximately 8,000 residents. Every shop we visited had the images of this devastation playing on their televisions. None of us comprehended this horrific event happening on the opposite side of the country, and yet it somehow felt like it was happening just down the street.

When the ship returned to Vancouver a few days later it was utter chaos, Mom and Dad were leaving to go home; they managed as they were flying within Canada. I did not leave the ship that day for fear of not being able to get back on board. In addition to most flights being grounded, seafaring travellers were affected as well. This was the biggest challenge that the Cruise Line had faced in all the years that I was with the company. Flights could not get in so guests could not connect to their next voyage. Guests could not get flights out so there was nowhere for them to go at the completion of their existing cruise. The company decided since we had the two ships in port, to let one set sail with the guests who did arrive for their Alaskan cruise, and the other would stay in Vancouver to house the guests who could not leave.

This may sound like a simple solution but embarkation at the best of times is challenging for all. I offered my assistance; however, I was reminded by the Hotel Director that I was on vacation. Nevertheless, I stayed in crew areas all day and then went upstairs the following morning. Things were so crazy that I insisted that they let me assist at least with the background work and they did. Understandably, under these circumstances, it was chaos, but everyone, both guests and crew, gave it their all to make the best of this extremely unfortunate situation.

> **Beauty and travel surround me**
> **but life is so fragile and fleeting.**

Today as I look back, I realize that in addition to having been emotionally devastated by this horrific event, I still cannot comprehend that someone could even fathom dreaming up, never mind orchestrating, such an incredibly sophisticated grandiose plan in order to inflict so much death and devastation. It is just mind-boggling! I am baffled that hate can be so real that nations want to destroy other nations. I remember Mom saying to me, "This is the first war of your generation on North American soil." It was a pivotal moment in my life. The world had already become much smaller with all of my travels but now I could feel what it literally meant to call this world home. My eyes opened to all of the atrocities that had occurred around the globe in my parents' lifetime alone! What this incident did, unbeknownst to me at the time, it instantly sparked an interest in events and history worldwide!

Samba ...

‿℮ℓℓ‿

My request was honoured and not long after the completion of my Alaskan vacation, I returned as Group and Sales Coordinator and was about to embark on my first South American season. The first cruise departed from Fort Lauderdale and was a 14-night repositioning cruise to Valparaiso, Chile. This route included cruising the 51 miles through the Panama Canal. The ship entered the first set of locks in the morning where we were lifted 170 feet, and then we sailed into Gatun Lake. We continued through the waterways enjoying the beauty of the dense rainforests hoping to see one of the many species of wildlife that inhabit this incredible part of the world. A few hours later as we were enjoying a full commentary of the history of this grand engineering innovation, we were being lowered by the second set of locks. Shortly after exiting the canal in the early evening, we had the opportunity to enjoy a magnificent view, as we sailed past Panama City at sunset.

We visited some very unique ports of call, such as Colon, Panama; Puntarenas, Costa Rica; and Cartagena, Columbia; which was another port offering stunning views during sail in and sail away! My favourite stop just prior to going through the Canal is the San Blas Islands in Panama. It is comprised of 365 islands and cays (a low island or reef of sand or coral) scattered in a 100-square mile radius of which 49 islands are inhabited by the local Kuna Indians. This is one of the most unique experiences and should not to be missed when sailing to South America.

The most memorable part of our San Blas experience, and something definitely worth waking up early for, is the Panamanian locals coming out to greet the ship. Before the ship had even stopped to drop anchor, many small carved out wooden boats would surround the vessel. In each boat there was a family; a father holding a paddle to manoeuvre the tiny wobbly boat, a mother dressed in brightly coloured clothing and sometimes holding infants as well as small children with big smiles on their faces. They would all be looking up, greeting the guests and crew with cupped hands, containers, or upside down umbrellas in hopes of receiving small donations. The guests would toss coins, and on many occasions you would see some of the small children dive off their boats into the water to retrieve the stray coins that had missed their targets. Surely, this was one of the many travel memories etched in my heart.

Prior to tendering the guests ashore we would offload all the necessary food and beverage supplies to one of the smaller-uninhibited islands. Once all the previsions and crewmembers were ashore our guests would have the opportunity to spend a glorious day on the island complete with lunch, tropical drinks and of course five-star service provided by the officers, staff and crew. The guests could enjoy the warmth of the sunshine on the beach before cooling off with a swim in the crystal clear waters, or venture off for a short walk around the island while enjoying the peace and tranquility of this glorious setting which truly is paradise.

An option for the more adventurous would be to take a ride in a small dug out boat with one of the locals from a nearby island to visit their home. This is an opportunity to see how the Kuna Indians live.

I still have cherished memories of our local boat adventure just before Christmas many years ago. The trip to the small nearby island was followed by a tour around the village, compliments of our local captain. We were able to take in all the colourful sights, sounds and aromas. The local women were proudly displaying (and of course selling) their customary handmade goods just outside their small huts, which included molas, the traditional handmade textiles of their culture. The children were running and playing, smiling and waving, and food preparations were visible throughout the village. It was obvious from the energy that most were extremely thrilled by our visit.

Anne and I found a small restaurant; actually we were invited and escorted into a small hut by a charming gentleman we met along the way. The area had a straw roof and a dirt floor, housed three small tables with white plastic chairs and sat directly on the waterfront. It had no signage and no menus.

I remember what surprisingly stood out above all else was that here on this island paradise, in the middle of nowhere, and what felt like a million miles from home, stood a beautifully decorated *live* Christmas tree, complete with local handcrafted decorations!

So here we sat on this tiny island, in a small hut, on the waterfront in the archipelago de San Blas in December. What bliss being surrounded by blue skies, crystal clear turquoise water, with a colourful mola-themed Christmas tree, and enjoying the lunch special of the day – fresh caught lobster!

The second leg began in Valparaiso, Chile. Valparaiso is located approximately 70 miles south of Santiago. It is affectionately known as "Little San Francisco" by international sailors and historically was a magnet for European immigrants. The opening of the Panama Canal and the reduction of ship traffic was a financial blow to Valparaiso. Many families abandoned the city, however, over the past 15 years the city has been recovering, attracting artists and cultural entrepreneurs. Today thousands of visitors from around the world visit this labyrinth of cobbled alleys and colourful buildings painted in an array of different colours. It is a fantastic place to walk, explore and take sensational photos. One thing to note, the spectacular city hike and its breathtaking views are all uphill!

From Valparaiso we would sail around the southern tip of South America cruising past the scenic Chilean Fjords. Sailing through the Straits of Magellan and around Cape Horn we would visit the most southern tip of South America; Tierra del Fuego is an archipelago – a group of islands at South America's southernmost tip. The islands are shared by Chile and Argentina. Its windswept tundra, evergreens bent in accordance to the winds, snow-capped mountains and blue ice glaciers are a sight to behold. Ushuaia, Argentina; sometimes called "the End of the World," is a resort town on Isla Grande, the main island of Tierra del Fuego. Ushuaia is a gateway to the northern regions and Antarctica to the south. This is where I witnessed firsthand the real-life postcard picture of this charming western-like town. It nestles the coastline and is centered in front of a magnificent backdrop of massive snow-capped mountains. As the ship departed just before dusk and the city lights were coming on we had the opportunity to not only experience this spectacular picturesque sight but also its crystal clear refection in the calm Beagle Channel – stunning!

The final stop on our 14-night around the Horn cruise was Buenos Aires. It was our turn around port; we would then do the same cruise in reverse. After many visits throughout the season, I decided that this bustling cosmopolitan capital of Argentina was one of my favourite cities. It is a beautiful city with a heavy Spanish influence. The air is filled with romantic music, the ambiance is inviting, the food is mouth-watering and there is so much to see and do which places Buenos Aires towards the top on my list of beloved places.

Giannis had completed his mandatory schooling and was due to arrive in Buenos Aires on December 23rd. I waited patiently all day. It was 30 minutes prior to departure and

Giannis had not arrived. For those last 30 minutes I sat looking down the pier through the window, praying that he would catch the ship and that we would spend Christmas together. It was now five o'clock and time to set sail, Giannis had not arrived. I found out later that he had missed the second leg of his flight. Although sad, I counted my blessings that he was safe and that he would arrive a few days later. And he did arrive; however, his luggage with my gifts from him and his family did not, which left him very disappointed. Needless to say, I was ecstatically happy with *"my late gift,"* Giannis, he was all I needed, and he made New Year's Eve perfect! Unfortunately, despite our continued effort to locate his luggage, it was never found and the airline's payout was not of any comfort for lost treasures. Life did however go on and with time we did realize that it was only *stuff*.

Giannis and I enjoyed some stunning evenings in Buenos Aires; we dined on world famous Argentinean beefsteak dinners, tasted flavourful local wines and watched sultry authentic tango shows. I loved the city so much I considered purchasing some real estate, which was a nice idea but it didn't happen.

The highlighted cruise of the season was in February when we had three overnights in Rio de Janeiro for the world-renowned Rio Carnival. With my parents onboard I jumped at the opportunity to take in all the sights from Copacabana beach to Sugarloaf Mountain. We stood under the Christ the Redeemer statue atop Corcovado Mountain, which offered a breathtaking view of the city of Rio de Janeiro. We looked on and enjoyed the Samba Parade at the Sambadrome; a once in a lifetime opportunity and the wildest parade and party ever!

As we begun our journey around Cape Horn, I was reminded by the onboard chatter about rough seas in this area. Apparently, the ship the previous season had had a few encounters with Mother Nature. Fortunately for us we had calm seas for our entire South

Laura Goor

America season. I remember this contract as smooth sailing all around; the seas were calm, my relationships with the crew were very pleasant, work was a joy and my relationship with Giannis was great. Life was good!

72

Expansion ...

During the following two years I would cover vacation time for Managers. I would spend two months on one vessel, two months on another and then have vacation for two months myself. It was an incredible opportunity to visit and compare the various ships, meet new people, see more of this incredible world including Europe and North Africa, and it offered an excellent learning experience. I did eventually decide that it was time for me to settle down again so I requested to do an entire contract on one ship. My request was granted, I received a permanent ship and once again, I was back with my man.

When I began working for the cruise line we didn't have computer systems onboard, so all guest issues and concerns were written by hand into a log. We would record a guest concern such as, "Toilet not working stateroom 4031" in our logbook, leave half a page for follow up and then write the next log. Now, of course, computers do everything and despite the fact that it was not really all *that* long ago the memories seem, well, prehistoric and must be humorous for those who did not get to experience manual logbook entries firsthand. Over the first 12 years of my life onboard I got to personally witness how far and fast technology was developing. Well, something from high school paid off, I had learned how to type so I was able to navigate the various new onboard computer programs as they were introduced.

With time came more updates, amendments and changes. The sales aspect of the job initially entailed only eight hours of advertised desk time – *per cruise*! This allowed guests to come and see me to book their next cruise while onboard. As the demand grew, the Group and Sales position became two separate mandates and I opted to go with the sales arm of the position. Moving forward my full-time position would be Future Cruise Sales and the Loyalty Hostess, who was now responsible for our loyalty members and the VIPs, reported to me, making me also responsible for overseeing the loyalty program. I loved the job, the ships, the itineraries but most importantly the people.

People ...

When I began working for the cruise line, I remember thinking, I am going to be greeting and servicing some of the happiest people on earth. In my mind, who would not be ecstatic when taking a cruise? Well, as with any career working with the public, it is never static – every day, every interaction is different; you see it all! I would jokingly say that the family gave all the cranky relatives a holiday cruise. Which when translated meant; they were now ours to "deal" with while the families back home celebrated in peace.

When it comes to travelling, not much compares to experiencing your first cruise. It brought me such pleasure to see the sparkle in someone's eyes the moment they set foot on the gangway. They would be greeted with a heartfelt *"Welcome onboard"* and a crewmember would assist with their carry-on while they were being offered a glass of champagne. With live music playing in the background, the atmosphere was electric as our guest began the vacation of a lifetime.

I will never forget how my dad reacted on his first cruise as a guest. It was not his first time on a ship, as Dad's first experience was as a teen onboard a vessel sailing out of the Netherlands; he worked as a cook. From the second he arrived on board he was like a four-year old, in awe of absolutely everything around him. He was mesmerized by the surroundings, captivated by the ambiance, and enthralled by the sheer graciousness and service of the crew. He soaked it all up; the variety and abundance of foods, the cabin and its amenities, and the various lounges, pools and shows where he could further relax. I have photos of him going into the theatre and stopping for a photo op with the Cruise Director and the costumed dancers; he was beaming with utter delight, like a boy on his first date. I can safely say that the pleasure of just being out on a ship's deck breathing in the salty sea air, enjoying the warm Caribbean breezes and the sound of the waves dancing against the hull made my dad's heart sing!!

I chuckle knowing that my dad was proud that his daughter worked onboard as well. Notably, hours did not go by without someone coming up to me to say that they had met my dad. The crew enjoyed many laughs with my parents, helping to make their cruise an experience of a lifetime. My career and travels have introduced me to a wide variety of people from all over the world. They spoke many different languages; many spoke English as a second language, some spoke no English at all. I have learned to understand and respect the various cultures, religions, and languages. I grew in empathy as I heard their personal stories of hardships, wars, and so much more. I have worked with and have friends from war-torn and poverty-stricken regions around the globe. A world, which once upon a time, to me, was bigger than I could have ever comprehended, has now become much smaller than I could have imagined. My view of the world today is more unmediated, real and is now combined with firsthand heartbreaking accounts as well as many heart-warming tales, all which are etched into my heart.

I spent many glorious evenings with incredible people learning their unique life stories and accounts of this phenomenal world we live in. My dear friend and the ships' Loyalty Hostess, Roxanna, is of Romanian descent. It was the Christmas season and her first celebration away from home. As we were relaxing over drinks with a couple we had grown to know and adore over the years, Roxanna began to recount her days of Christmases past in Romania. She shared stories with us about growing up in a communist country. One heart-warming tale, which stood out for me, was her love for oranges and what they represented to her. Oranges were a sign of wealth and only accessible during Christmas, which was the only time a year that she ate them. She told us that today the aroma of an orange immediately transports her home. We all knew that being away from home and being an only child who would be missing her family, that this was going to be a very difficult celebration for her.

On Christmas day Roxanna came into work and was in tears. I asked, "What on earth" and she told me that this morning when she opened her cabin door, to her surprise and delight there was a big basket filled with oranges and a Merry Christmas note from the guests. She said that she dropped to her knees and hugged the basket as hard as she would have hugged her parents and cried. For the next few days Roxanna thoroughly enjoyed eating oranges while reminiscing of Christmases back home with her family. She freely gave love and hugs to the guests in appreciation for the incredible gesture of sincere love. For me, Roxanna's journey was not only the highlight of that holiday season, but remained in my heart for many Christmases to come.

As a Canadian-born child, you could say that I was isolated in my knowledge of the world and world events; I was shielded, grew up in a safe and comfortable bubble. I did watch the nightly news; nevertheless, I did not truly grasp the reality of what was transpiring in the world. It was as if I was watching a movie; I had become numb to all the images of war, famine and the atrocities in the world. My travels have helped deepen my understanding of our world, the people and the animals that inhabit this beautiful planet. I now feel personally invested; I know people from all over the world and today I am affected deeply, whether it is a natural disaster, violence, war or injustices that infect their lands.

I have found a balance; in addition to my interest in world news, politics, global affairs, travel and discovery, I am interested in personal growth stories and reality shows that showcase life's miracles. I have discovered stories of hope, moments of inspiration and have seen challenges overcome by opening my eyes to life.

Looking back, I wish I had kept a journal. I personally witnessed or have been told of some crazy incidents that could have been a book on its own and I learned first hand the true meaning of "don't sweat the small stuff" as they say.

December 27th, 2004... It was the day after the devastating Indian Ocean tsunami; 230,000 plus people in 14 countries were affected.

This day we were scheduled to dock in Key West but due to inclement weather we were unable to get into the port. At the Guest Relations desk an irate guest was screaming at the top of his lungs "This is a disaster!" It just so happened that his tirade landed on the ears of the Hotel Director who very calmly and politely said, "No sir, what happened yesterday was a disaster, this sir, is an inconvenience."

No matter *what* happens in our lives, it can be looked at from different perspectives. Some will sweat the little things and allow them to ruin an entire vacation. Others see that things cannot be changed, accept that it is what it is, and make the most of the situation under the circumstances.

I will never forget the final words of the evening from a comedian who was performing on the ship; he said to the audience at the end of the show..."If I have seriously offended you in any way... you really need to lighten up!"

Expectations...

⟨ℓℓ⟩

Travel with no expectations
and surely you will be pleasantly surprised!

This is just another one of the great lessons I have learned from my 20 years at sea and travelling the world.

They say that you can discern a person's character by one or more of the following situations: how they deal with lost luggage or a long string of knotted Christmas lights, how they treat a waiter or how they react to rain. Ah, I bet you know someone like this or you may be that person! When working with the public you experience all manner of personalities and then the individual moves along for example to the next counter or store; however, not on a cruise ship.

It begins with the desire to travel; we sit back and envision the perfect vacation. In our mind's eye, we see our flights being on time, luggage arriving when we do, the perfect temperature, blue skies, warm seas, no lineups, beautiful hotels, delicious meals, and amazingly friendly service, right? In life, we continuously set ourselves up for failure by expecting everything to go as planned. Sometimes we are disappointed, and for most, it will be short-lived. For some, these challenges, unfortunately, put a real damper on their vacation or even on their lives in general and they beg the question "Why me?" "Why now?" or even just "Why?" Unfortunately, there is no good answer to the "Why" that will make them feel better in their difficult situation. The solution is not changing vendors for better service, as they are temporarily confined onboard a floating city. The solution is acceptance of, not resistance to, the circumstances. I realized after years of assisting people with changing and challenging circumstances that our quality of life all depends on how we react to what life sends our way.

Resistance is what causes pain, not the situation itself.

Cruise after cruise each guest stateroom is the same, the food is the same and so are other amenities; however, guest reactions range from one end of the spectrum to the other. What one person thinks is out of this world, and reacts with jubilation; another will not have the same experience and meet it with a very different reaction. It is the reaction that causes the drama in our lives, not the circumstances themselves. Does this mean that we have to smile and accept everything in life? No of course not. However, if we develop an attitude that everything is not always going to be perfect, and things can and occasionally will be *different*, it makes life a lot easier and more pleasurable to deal with. I have always said that if it wasn't for the adverse weather, we wouldn't appreciate the warmth and sunshine. I believe this analogy goes for just about everything in life and it is worth practicing regularly.

Let's be real, we have no control over the timing of our flights, the delivery of our luggage, whether it shines or rains and to think otherwise would be unrealistic. As soon as we learn to stop expecting the max and go with the current instead of against it, live in the moment, and accept that right now *it is what it is*, things start to flow much better than when we have unrealistic expectations.

During my four seasons cruising Northern Europe where we

could experience Canadian winter-like weather conditions in the middle of summer, our motto was, "If it doesn't rain, it's a beautiful day!"

Adjustment...

⟿

Working on a cruise ship involves adjustments from the moment you board to the completion of your contract. Cruise ship employment can be an extremely social event or it can be a very lonely experience. Those who have been at sea for an extended period have probably experienced some of both.

Talk about a huge extended family that you never knew you had until you board a ship as a member of the crew. As in every family, there are all kinds of personalities and imagine an 800 plus crew count on a smaller vessel, living in close proximity and getting acquainted with each other. This is a terrific opportunity to meet people whether at work, in the corridors, during meal times or in the crew lounges. The crew, for the most part, consists of naturally outgoing, energetic and pleasant individuals. New hires are skilled, upbeat, enthusiastic and helpful and those qualities are usually seen both while on and off duty. If you come into this working environment with these qualities, in my opinion, you can't lose. It may take some time to bond with others until you feel that you truly fit in, but with some genuine effort, you can be a part of this large diverse family.

On the newer larger ships crew counts go into the thousands; this makes for some tight living quarters. The majority of the crew-members have roommates; a good roommate and life onboard can be fun, get a problematic person and of course life can be hell.

It is not against regulations to bring someone home; however, if the roommate does not agree then other arrangements must be made, it is just a matter of courtesy. You do not have to like or agree with everyone but you can always appreciate someone, learn something and you might even make a new friend. Unfortunately, some roomies don't speak up and therefore endure the anguish of waking up to an extra body in the cabin. I had been very fortunate that for the majority of my years onboard, I had a roommate with a boyfriend, leaving me with the cabin to myself, or I had a boyfriend with his own cabin, leaving my cabin to my roommate.

What I have learned from living onboard a ship is how you adjust will determine your experiences away from your family and home.

#Metoo ...

⟡

When I began "Twenty Years at Sea" this chapter did not exist. A friend who knows me well asked me why I was not covering such a relevant and important topic; she insisted that I should. My sincere response at the time was, "There's too much good stuff to share, so why should I write about that and bad things happen everywhere." Why cover sexual assault? The reason I changed my mind is to shed light on a widespread problem that infiltrates not only Hollywood but also every part of the workforce where men with power or influence can and will wield control over women. I honestly believe that what we see in the media is only the tip of the iceberg and that millions of women will never get their say – so I will now speak up.

It was early in my career when the assault took place and years later it was revealed to me that I was not alone. We did not swap stories, nor did I speak out until many years later. All but one of us, besides telling a couple of friends, did nothing. I know the immediate question is "Why on earth would we remain silent after being assaulted?" I can only answer for myself. Shame and embarrassment kept me silent. I blamed myself, how could I allow myself to get into such a situation in the first place and I know the other women felt the same.

Here is my story …

During the early days of my career, we did not have televisions in our cabins. Accordingly, we entertained ourselves with parties. I lived in the corridor with the dancers and since we had the biggest cabin, we usually hosted the neighbourhood parties. One evening my neighbour and I were chatting and he said, "There's this guy onboard that I really like but because I have a straight roommate, we can't spend time together." I knew his roommate very well and I said "My roommate is gone for the night so why doesn't your roommate stay in her bunk." I did not for one single second think anything of my offer, as we were all friends. Once the party was over and the crew left, I went into my bunk and 'John' took the upper bunk. In my mind the night was over; well, he did not and decided that he was going to take advantage of my intoxicated state and came into my bunk. A struggle ensued, I lost, and he won. From the next day forward, we pretended nothing happened and I for years did not say a word. The other victims had also invited male crewmembers into their rooms with the belief that they would not be assaulted by a peer.

Working on a cruise ship is akin to college or university. A lot of people, parties, and alcohol can be a recipe for incidents such as these to occur. Men and women should remain alert so that these scenarios do not happen. I have always said to my staff, "Do *not* get yourself into a situation – being alone with someone – where this can happen; until you get to know someone well enough to want to be with them, stay in a public place." I know it is easier said than done but this can and will assist with these situations being avoided. Moreover, in a case where someone has been assaulted, it is important that all individuals know that they can comfortably come forth, without shame or embarrassment; tell his or her story, so that the perpetrator can be prosecuted.

My regret to this day is that I will never know if he harmed anyone else and that I will have to live with.

Safety...

~elle~

Living and working onboard a ship is not for everyone. Some find it very confining and unlike a hotel, this establishment floats around on large bodies of water and at times you are days away from land. Safety is of the utmost importance and it is therefore the responsibility of the crew to assist in the unlikely event of an emergency. The modern vessels are equipped with the latest safety features and after each embarkation a simulated boat drill is mandatory for all guests and crew. The thought of something actually going wrong; a collision, terrorist attack or fire onboard was incomprehensible, even to many of the crew. Despite what we felt, all of the crew undergoes extensive safety training, which is repeated every time we return from vacation and further training is provided throughout the contract. In addition, the ship, the cruise company and the crew are responsible for passing Coast Guard inspections worldwide.

As important as safety is, on this one particular occasion there was a humorous side. I was performing my duties on embarkation day; my responsibilities included ensuring that all guests had their lifejackets on correctly and that they were entering into the correct muster (gathering) station. I assisted a gentleman with putting on his life jacket; at the time I thought nothing of it because this is what I did every cruise for years. What is funny about this story is on the following morning I arrived in my office to find a sketch, drawn by the onboard character artist, on my desk – the picture says it all – priceless!

Onboard...

~ele~

I arrived at work every day without having to deal with traffic, snow, subways or crowds of people. The coffee is made and on the way to the office I would say hello to everyone; almost everyone I met knew me, and most greeted me by name. When I arrived at the office, the window behind me had a different view every day of the week. Now that is extraordinary! I would work for a few hours and then eat a gourmet lunch. I would then return to the office, work for a few more hours, followed by a dinner break with meals no less extravagant than lunch. Back to work again for a couple of hours and then off for the evening.

Nine pm... Decision time, what should I do for the evening? Get away from the world to be alone or get together with friends to chat the night away? If I did not go yesterday and I was feeling energetic, it would be off to the gym. If not the gym, then maybe I would go to see a Broadway show or the various artists who performed nightly in the theatre. If we had already seen the show or felt like just kicking back we may have opted for a glass of wine in one of the many lounges. Another evening option would be to sit back, relax in bed and watch a good movie or channel flick, and watch a few bad ones!

Imagine strolling on the deck under a moving night sky. This was a favourite pastime of mine; nothing but water all around, breathing in the salty air while listening to the waves bouncing off the vessel. A special treat would be clear skies revealing millions of stars sparkling in the night.

I had the opportunity and pleasure to be on deck for most of our sail aways. Some memorable departures in addition to Alaska, St. Thomas and Cartagena were from Naples, Italy. About an hour after departing, we would sail by the island of Capri at the exact time that the sun was making its descent; this was stunning! We also cruised by the small island of Stromboli off the coast of Sicily where there is an active volcano with plumes of steam becoming visible just before sunset and after sunset the volcano glowed red in the dying light. For this reason, Stromboli is nicknamed the "Lighthouse of the Mediterranean." A sail away from any port is always beautiful; as is passing a picturesque island or a majestic landmass.

There were so many memorable strolls and sail aways during my many years at sea.

Entertainment ...

As members of the crew, we are responsible for the well-being of our guests, from embarkation to debarkation ensuring that they are greeted with a smile, well-fed and entertained. What about the hard-working crew; I believe that if we were left to our own vices there would be chaos or some may have died from boredom!

We had what was then referred to as a Crew Welfare Coordinator onboard each ship to watch over the crew's well-being. That individual was responsible for organizing crew events; there were tournaments for board games, ping-pong, volleyball and basketball. Sometimes if a sister ship was in port with us they would arrange a tournament between the crew from both vessels. Everyone onboard had access to the gym facilities; officers and staff could enjoy the guest gym during after hours and on port days and the crew had access to the crew gym located in the crew area. On a more social level, wine and cheese nights, theme parties, karaoke, and movie nights would keep the boredom at bay. Shore side activities and crew tours were available to help us expand our knowledge of the areas we travelled. In my opinion, the highlight of ship life was having the opportunity to go ashore whether to explore on our own or venture out with a group. Since we did not have television onboard back in the early years, there were complimentary video rentals of movies and TV series. Not to be forgotten, Mass and Bible class were available to the faithful. I believe all of these offerings kept most of us grounded during our extended stay onboard.

At various points throughout the years, no alcohol was permitted in the cabins, in order to deter people from having cabin parties. As employees work all hours of the day or night, there are always people sleeping and there is nothing worse than trying to sleep while listening to your neighbours "live it up." Out of respect for others, these parties are frowned upon and if security is called to break one up, the crewmembers may be reprimanded. That does not mean that there were no cabin parties!

Thanks to duty-free, alcohol and cigarettes are offered at a reduced rate; the bar options onboard for crew consist of the smoking and the non-smoking bar. In the olden days, there was the officer's dayroom where you could smoke and socialize; the non-smokers referred to this area as the smoke pit. At 10 pm the smoking bar transforms into the crew disco, where a crewmember would volunteer to DJ. The night usually started off quiet but by closing the dance floor was packed.

For pest control reasons, no open food was allowed in the crew cabins. All our meals onboard were complimentary; breakfast, lunch and dinner, coffee breaks and midnight snacks. The ship ran on fuel and the crew was fuelled by food! We were spoiled; in the past, we had an Officer's mess, Staff mess, Crew mess and Indonesian mess. Nowadays the focus is one mess serving healthy cuisine, one offers international foods and another offers fast foods such as hamburgers and hot dogs. Special meals, buffets and BBQ's are prepared periodically for holidays, celebrations and staff appreciation days.

Working any position on a cruise ship has its challenges, but with the help of a positive mindset and various activities, my Twenty Years at Sea weren't so bad and I will say it again – Life was Good!

Explore ...

From the moment I set foot on board I had a yearning to see everything there was to see ashore, no matter where in the world we were. I seized the opportunity to be a tour escort whenever possible and I loved to just walk and explore the ports of call. I have always had a good sense of time and of direction; I would venture off just about anywhere and everywhere and I most often would do it alone. Exploring somewhere new and not knowing what lies just beyond the horizon or around the next corner is one of life's best gifts. Exploring is a gift of independence, freedom, peace, and excitement all wrapped up in one!

Not all the crew shared my enthusiasm for exploration; I was in the habit of regularly asking others "Are you going out today?" The general answer would be, "To do what?" or "Why, we're here all the time?" Others would be too hung-over from partying and sleep the time away. Some of the crew focused on saving their money to send back home to their families and chose to stay onboard. I have always believed that a walk, or even a trip to the beach, if not free, costs very little and even a short time spent off the ship in these exotic ports felt like an entire day off. My adventurous nature combined with my curiosity has allowed me to experience some of the most incredible sights that this world has to offer. I have lived out experiences that were far beyond my wildest dreams.

In St. Petersburg, Russia, I strolled through the streets

admiring the architecture of iconic monuments and buildings. I was mesmerized by the beauty of the churches, palaces and museums, all adorned with colourful mosaics. I experienced a ballet in the State Hermitage Museum, which is located inside the Winter Palace of Empress Catherine The Great. I stood in Red Square, Moscow, the location of Saint Basil's Cathedral, the Kremlin, Lenin's Tomb, the Kremlin graveyard and the State History Museum, all places that I had only read about until then. I rode the Russian subway system; it is the world's deepest and has the most opulent stations anywhere in the world. I have navigated and negotiated my way through the markets in Tunis and Agadir and was awed by the snake charmers in the Marrakesh city square. I will never forget climbing the ancient steps to the Acropolis to be inspired by the temples and buildings of a bygone era. The Acropolis also offered a beautiful view of the city of Athens and the Mediterranean Sea off in the distance. I cannot forget France and my visit to the Eifel Tower as well as Notre Dame Cathedral in Paris; it was magnifique! London offered up Big Ben, Westminster Abbey and bangers and mash, another amazing adventure. I snorkelled the Great Barrier Reef in Australia. This truly was a world like no other; it is the world's largest coral reef system, larger than the Great Wall of China – imagine that. In addition to the glaciers of Alaska, I witnessed black bears fishing for salmon in the icy rivers. I experienced the wonders of the Great Pyramids of Giza and rode a camel in the desert. These are just some of the places and a few of the sights I have been fortunate to have had the opportunity to explore during my travels.

It is inconceivable what *we can* accomplish in our lives; the endless opportunities which come our way *if* we just follow our heart and take risks but most importantly – take action! What is even more incredible is not only *can* our dreams come true, but we can also have experiences in our lives which *are beyond* our wildest dreams if we will just step out and onto our path.

Europe ...

Throughout my career I have often been asked, where is your favourite place on earth? This has always been a very difficult question for me to answer. I truly do love and appreciate all that I have had the opportunity to see, experience and embrace. Nevertheless, I have chosen my top three.

Santorini, Greece... Two days after attending a delightful wedding in Trikala, a small city in north-western Greece, Giannis and I travelled by ferry from Piraeus to Santorini. We took the trip with the bride and groom. It was an overnight trip, Giannis and I chose not to pay the extra for a cabin and instead decided to bunk on benches on the open deck! We both agreed never again, certain things in life are worth paying for – a cabin on a Greek ferry being one of them. Once my achy body could stretch out, I looked up to see a beautiful clear blue sky but it was when I turned around, I gasped! I had no idea what to expect, as I never do my homework before travelling. There before me, as high up as the eye could see was a vertical rugged landscape, similar to the red cliffs in Utah. However, here the landscape was beige, brown and white, and ascended from the blue Aegean Sea. At first glance, it seemed that the cliffs were covered with snow. As we sailed closer it became clear that it was the stunning whitewashed cubiform houses with blue shutters, which clung to the side of these magnificent cliffs.

The contrast of colours was breathtaking; blue sky above, crystal clear waters reflecting the colour of the sky and nestled in between this vastness are the towns of Fira and Oia.

We docked at the pier and stood at the base looking straight up at this incredible landmass. The bus we boarded zigzagged its way on a narrow path up this great wall to the top. Once there, the view was no less spectacular than our approach to the island. The landscape is speckled with small white towns and the sea is visible in all directions. Dotting the turquoise waters are sailboats, ferries and small fishing boats all going about their lives and from where we stood you can see the volcanic island of Nea Kameni in the distance.

Santorini was formed by a volcanic eruption in the 16th century BC and can be best described as a group of islands consisting of Thíra, Thirassiá, Asproníssi, Palea and Nea Kaméni. This island grouping is still an active volcano. A part of the beauty of this natural wonder is that the volcano's crater is in the sea. Imagine soaking in the view of crystal clear waters while perched on the rim of this active volcano in the middle of the sea at sunset!

We spent a week in this lover's paradise. Beautiful black sand beaches lining the blue Aegean Sea, narrow streets and small towns to explore with charming local personalities filled our days. My favourite pastime was to unwind with Greek music in the background and chilled Santorini wine while sitting at a taverna.

Whether it is the view from above, the warm inviting waters or the Santorini sunsets, this romantic get-a-way was difficult to leave; so Giannis and I stayed behind and the honeymooners went on to Mykonos. I decided during that trip that this was my absolute favourite place on earth, and today after many more visits over the years, this has never changed.

Istanbul, Turkey... I absolutely love this magnificent city – the city of two continents! It ranks as the seventh-largest city by population in the world and the largest in Europe. Half of the city is located in Europe and the other half is in Asia. Istanbul is connected by the Bosporus Bridge; a suspension bridge that resembles, although slightly smaller, the Golden Gate Bridge. The ship sails into the city by way of the Bosporus Strait; the approach offers a breathtaking view of the city on either side. Upon arrival she turns around and docks in the center of the city, providing an extraordinary 360-degree view for all onboard to enjoy. Off the stern, you can view the bridge, Topkapi Palace, Hagia Sophia Museum, and the Blue Mosque all standing above a spectacularly beautiful bustling city crammed with buildings, narrow streets, and mosques. The waterways are littered with tiny fishing boats and hundreds of small ferries and water taxis transporting people to and from various parts of the city. As incredible as this view is during the day, it is dazzling at night. In addition to the bridge joining two continents, it also joins cultures and people.

I appreciate Istanbul for its diversity, which makes it so incredibly rich and beautiful, and gives you an appreciation for the peoples of our world. This city houses 16 million people; you will see everything from women wearing Niqabs and Hijabs, men in their various local attire, to men, woman and children in blue jeans, t-shirts, Nikes and baseball caps. Since I was working on ships and returning to ports repeatedly, I had the opportunity to get to know these foreign destinations well enough to venture out on my own to explore and soak in the local culture. I do not recommend that people who are exploring Istanbul for the first time to do so on their own. The city is massive, extremely busy and very easy to get lost in if you do not have your bearings. In addition, there is plenty to see and traffic is a nightmare so the best way to make the most of this port is to do an organized ship tour.

It was always a thrill wandering throughout Istanbul. I have explored the many corners of this grand city, from the steep cobblestone streets with its local shops and markets to the lavish maze within Grand Bazaar to Taxim Square, which is a modern main street with high-end shops and coffee houses. In the evenings the dark narrow back streets of Taxim are packed with one small restaurant after another overflowing with patrons. The local music blaring from every corner, combined with the smell of grilled street food in the air, and a warm magical night is a must-have experience in this lifetime. If you desire a more spiritual cleansing experience, a Turkish bath is a must-try!

I have developed an affinity for the warm, gentle, kind-hearted Turkish people and the blend of cultures in their country.

Venice, Italy... My first visit to Venice was during my Contiki Tour of Europe, which surprisingly at that time did not make an impression on me. However, as we sailed past Piazza San Marco (St Mark's Square) and the Grand Canal I gasped at the awe-inspiring 360-degree view of the city; it was at that moment I instantly fell in love with Venice. The true beauty of this amazing city is that you can traverse Venice. It takes about forty-five minutes on foot from Piazzale Roma, at the top, to Piazza San Marco at the bottom, allowing you to see and sense the ancient history of this city.

The city is comprised of 117 islands, built on a lagoon and is connected by canals while linked by 400 bridges, Venice is truly a feat of engineering. I believe the fun begins once you venture off the beaten path. You most certainly will get lost in the maze of streets and alleys as you explore and find your bearings. Venice was our homeport at the time, and it took me most of the summer to finally locate the famous historical Venetian Jewish Ghetto which is situated somewhere in the middle of this incredible maze. This is where Jews were forced to live by the Government of the Venetian Republic in 1516 and is the oldest Jewish Ghetto in the world. It should be noted that the Ghetto was dissolved in 1797 by the conquering French army. Some of my most memorable days and evenings of exploration and photography were in Venice. My goal is always to take photos without people in them, so if the crowd went left, I went right! The highlight for most visitors is enjoying the sights and sounds of Venice via the canals on a Gondola ride and although it may appear to be a little touristy, it really is an impressive and relaxing way to see the sights. After enjoying a stroll or gondola ride through the streets and/or canals of Venice, my personal recommendation is to find an outdoor pizzeria in any one of narrow streets and relax while giving in to Italy's mouth-watering pizza and extraordinary ambiance. Another must-see along the way is to sit in Piazza San Marco and enjoy the music, the people and the pigeons while eating gelato (Italian ice cream), enjoying an espresso or a glass of vino.

Getting lost is truly not a bad thing. Around every corner is guaranteed another stunning piece of architecture to behold and to me, taking the road less travelled is always full of delightful surprises.

I love all of Europe! However, Greece tops the list, Turkey is my second and Italy ranks third. All three countries are so awe-inspiring because of the people, culture, history, architecture, local customs, and romantic languages. Along with aromatic foods and local vintages, this makes all three countries my go-to places for inspiration! These are countries that have stirred my heart, taken me on an adventure, or reminded me how small our world really is.

However, that does not mean that the rest of Europe is not worth seeing, I would go back to visit anywhere in Europe in a heartbeat!

Life ...

~ele~

If you stop, and be still for a moment, take a *deep* breath and *really* think about it – life is incredible! Every one of us is like a snowflake – unique and so are our individual life stories. Be it so, it is interesting how much time and energy we give to fitting in when we were designed to stand out. Once I began to review the stages of my life, my challenges and accomplishments, I saw an evolution and whether the personal growth was big or small, depending on the circumstance – I evolved. I began to have a better understanding of the world around me and within myself.

Following are 10 simple truths I have learned.

1.   It is of no consequence to you what *others* do with their lives. Rather, it is what *you* do with yours. Do what is truly right for you.

2.   It does not matter where you have been or what you have done, today *is* a brand new day and today you *can* be a brand new you.

3.   The past is exactly that – the past – and it is done and gone. You cannot get it back; there are no do-overs to make changes. Nothing good comes out of suffering over what was. The only relevance to your past is that it was your

path to today. Be aware of past lessons learned, cherish your fond memories and move forward.

4. Your future is not a reality yet; planning for your future is sound advice, however worrying about the things you have no control over will not accomplish a thing. Live in the moment and ask yourself "What can I do right now, right this minute to enhance my life?"

5. The unknown is one of life's greatest gifts. You should welcome it, embrace it and enjoy the ride.

6. Life is like a play and with every day a new act is written and you can choose how that act is going to play out. I say let us make today a great act!

7. Simplify your life! Truth be told, we spend so much of our quality time complicating things thus causing ourselves much unnecessary grief. Clear out the clutter and go with the flow.

8. It is what it is! What is done is done; replaying past situations in your mind will only cause you pain and suffering. Accepting the past will put you on the path to healing.

9. Learn to love yourself, unconditionally. We cannot possibly love anyone else nor can anyone else love us if we do not love ourselves first!

10. Enjoy your own company. You can share a lot with yourself when you are introspective! Make quality alone time for yourself.

The outcome of your life is based on the choices you make along the way. If you stop and seriously think about it, your life is *all* about choices. Every moment of every day, in everything you do, you make conscious or unconscious decisions. From what time you wake, what foods you eat, your activities, to your lifestyle.

Are you going to live 365 days
or are you going to live one day, 365 times?

Begin your day with reflective thoughts. Reflect on the choices you made yesterday. Did you have a great day? Did you make the right decisions? If not, is your inner voice telling you that you could have done some things differently? If so – how are you going to react today? The same way you did yesterday, receiving the same undesired outcome, or are you consciously going to try a new approach - a different act for today?

Indulge ...

. ℓℓ

Prior to working on a cruise ship, I could never have imagined going to a spa and having a therapeutic massage. During the early years of my career on ships, I knew spa services were available onboard and the occasional guest raved about the results. However, the thought of getting partially undressed and massaged was something that I never envisioned would become a part of my lifestyle.

About five years into my career, the spa manager requested that I be a model on embarkation days for reflexology (foot massage) and facials so I decided to give it a try. Over the years I have slowly expanded my comfort zone, thus allowing me to experience various treatments from full body deep tissue massages, to seaweed wraps and hot stones massages. I have to chuckle looking back on it all now, especially at my change of beliefs. Once you have a therapeutic massage, you wonder how you survived so many years without indulging. Tension builds up in our bodies in areas that we cannot even imagine, and we don't know that it's there until a massage therapist identifies the areas of tension build-up. The experience of having these problem areas worked on is incredible. Most companies today have a massage therapy package included in their insurance program and I believe we all should make it a part of our lives on a regular basis, especially if our insurance covers it. I remember asking the therapist one day,

"What happens to those of us who do not get these treatments?" to which he replied, "This is why so many people have stress-related issues that turn into more serious health problems."

A therapeutic message has you feeling totally relaxed and rejuvenated, feeling better than you could have ever imagined, it is truly amazing and life is too short not to indulge in this luxury.

Farewell ...

، ℓℓ~

As I sat in the St. Kitts airport waiting for my flight to Miami for a business meeting, I took the opportunity to reflect on my past contracts. It had, at this point, been about 10 years of working in the cruise industry and the ship I was leaving was being sold. I felt compelled to address an email to my colleagues before my departure.

Dearest All,

I'm not usually one to send goodbyes (I much prefer to sneak out quietly) but this is a very special farewell.

It has been an incredible past five years (and yes a few contracts prior to that as well), I am finally saying goodbye, packing up and moving on (some said it could never be :-))))).

I have spent a big part of my career here onboard, in various positions, so I don't have to tell any of you how tough it is for me to finally say goodbye, knowing it will probably be the last time on this vessel.

I just want to thank you all for making this time in my life so special. It has been an honour going through the past half-decade here onboard, leaving me with fond memories, which I will treasure always!

Please welcome Elsa; I know I'm leaving her in very good hands. It's the accomplishments that show who the true stars are and I've been blessed to work with the best!

I wish you all smooth sailing and continued success. I so look forward to meeting and working with you all again somewhere down the road.

Take Care, Luv you guys!

Although I was sad to say goodbye to some very dear friends, I knew that it was time for me to make a change and to move on. I had spent two summer seasons in Alaska, three glorious summer seasons in the Mediterranean and five winter seasons in the Caribbean, sailing out of Baltimore, Galveston, and San Juan.

The past five years saw me transfer to be with Giannis and witness many personal and professional events, which have given me an enlightened perspective on life. As I sat in the airport I gave thought to my relationship with Giannis. After seven and a half years we mutually agreed to go our separate ways. We had had a falling out over a difference of opinion, which sent me to my cabin for a few days. When we finally sat down to discuss the events, he confessed that he wanted children; he recently turned thirty and was feeling the draw to begin a family. We had discussed marriage on numerous occasions, however, we could never come to an agreement regarding having kids. I was older and desired to continue working, travelling and seeing the world. Even his mother's generous offer to help raise the kids while we were on ships was not enough to make me change my mind. I could not see myself coming home to Greece and to a child who spoke fluent Greek and possibly no English. That vision still makes me chuckle! At that time my offer to Giannis was "Can we have cats instead?" He looked at me with his adoring eyes, puckered his lips and said no.

I believe that as the years passed we both thought that the other would change their mind regarding having kids, but neither of us did. My mother said to me "I don't care what you do, as long as you do it because *you* want to and not because someone else wants you to." That statement got me thinking; I knew Giannis would make a wonderful father, but I also knew deep down that I did not want children and that I would only be doing it for him.

We both had truly fallen in love with each other, which made our parting even more difficult. After our relationship ended we continued working onboard the same ship and surprisingly we helped each other get through the breakup. It was an interesting healing process; we would each take turns crumbling, and the other would be supportive. Twenty plus years later, Giannis is still one of my dearest friends. He attained what he wanted in life; he has a beautiful wife, is a father to two precious daughters and a son and I am truly thrilled for them all. Giannis will always hold a special place in my heart. As for me – even though I am still single, I have confidence that someday, somewhere, my turn will come and I will experience true love once again.

I boarded the plane and as we were taking off I looked over the aisle and through the window, and there she was, my beloved ship, perfectly centered in the window. The plane then turned around so the ship was now visible through my own window. As a final farewell to my beloved, the plane then did a complete circle around the vessel where I was in awe of her once again for one last time.

Relationships ...

"The love boat promises something for everyone..." was part of the lyrics to a sitcom from the 70s, and I would sing that internally every time I saw what appeared to be a new crew romance. Crew love, romance and relationships onboard are topics that could hold their own in a book! As you can well appreciate the crew cannot fraternize with guests under any circumstances, ever, as this can lead to serious accusations, job loss or criminal charges.

Loneliness is possibly one of the worst feelings and when you are confined to a ship for long periods it can be debilitating if you do not form relationships. This, unfortunately, happens with some of the crew. Everyone onboard has a few things in common; they are a long way from home, they are with people they do not know and they all work very hard. It becomes more difficult if you share a cabin and have no real alone time to unwind.

So what really goes on between the crew? We are told that what is allowed is whatever happens between two consenting adults. Nevertheless, it is strongly emphasized during training that consenting does not mean under the influence of alcohol. So what brings the crew together? Initially, the desire to spend quality time with others, release stress and pass the time while floating around at sea. A sense of comradery takes away the sting of loneliness and relationships begin to form quickly. As a result, you observe all manner of affairs from drunken one-night stands to serious relationships. Life onboard is like Vegas, "What happens on a cruise ship, stays on a cruise ship!"

Most crewmembers are outgoing, adventurous, and gregarious professionals, who just happen to enjoy a good time. So does everyone meet Mr. or Ms. Right, fall madly in love and live happily ever after? No, of course not. However, I believe in honesty. Being honest with your partner about your needs and intentions is beneficial in facing the challenges of an onboard romance.

The best-case scenario for a shipboard romance usually means from the onset of the romance to the end of the contract or the day when the first of the two is signing off for vacation. On sign-off day, they promise to keep in touch and hope and envision that their next contract will put them on the same ship. A few do manage to work together again, however, most couples, after shedding a few tears and parting ways, email briefly and then the relationship fades, leaving fond memories. Usually one if not both find a new companion on their next contract. I have witnessed many friends who have fallen in love, gotten married and had children to live happily ever after. This notwithstanding, there have been children conceived because of shipboard romances and these mothers have carried on as single parents.

The lifestyle on ships does bring heartbreaks but it also offers the opportunity to experience many and different types of relationships, if you wish. An onboard romance gives you the chance to live in the moment, no worries about the past or future. While onboard you don't have to worry about what family members think about your choice of partner. Accordingly, your relationships, for the most part, are "current affairs" which is something that land life doesn't offer so easily or abundantly. As soon as two people have been seen twice together in public they are considered a couple and the topic of hot new gossip. The novelty, however, wears off three days later; by then it is "old news."

Vacations ...

◦℮℮◦

Working on a cruise ship is not a nine-to-five, five days a week and two weeks' vacation kind of a job. The crew work seven days a week for three to seven month stretches depending on their position. For some, it can be hard to comprehend such a work model, but I believe if you set your mind to it, have good friends and support, you can adapt. The payoffs to such a career are great; you get to travel the world while getting paid, and vacation time is normally two months – not many have that luxury!

The call to onboard life is different for everyone. Many crew-members work to support their spouses, children or parents back home. While onboard they work very hard, save every penny and look forward to the day they sign off to go home to be with their families. Likewise, many are single and choose this work-travel lifestyle to tour the world. Another amazing aspect of ship life is that you form friendships with people from countries all over the world. These friendships accordingly give you the opportunity to see the globe through the eyes of locals rather than visiting as a tourist. Through my travels, I have come to realize not only how small this world really is but, if given the opportunity to explore it and the people on it, what an extraordinary education it provides!

As I mentioned Greece ranks as my top vacation destination and what made it even better was I had Giannis as my personal tour guide. When I had the opportunity to vacation with him in his small village in the north of Greece, we took our time and explored the surrounding areas. I have toured the picturesque port city of Kavalla in the north down to Thessaloniki, Greece's second largest city on the eastern coast. While in Trikala, we had the opportunity to see the six Meteora Monasteries. Meteora means suspended in the air; these masterpieces were built high upon the top of breathtaking rock formations. I have to say my breath was taken away, yet another time, by this serene and mystical holy place.

While we were in Greece for Giannis's friends' wedding we took a drive to Athens. We drove along the southern coast enjoying the many small villages along the way before joining the honeymoon couple in Santorini. We decided to stay on the island a bit longer thus missing my opportunity to experience Mykonos on that trip. Luckily, I have since returned to Mykonos with the cruise ships many times. Mykonos, although not built upon the cliffs like Santorini is just as charming, with its narrow colourful streets, whitewashed houses, unique shops as well as quaint tavernas and coffee shops. A fabulous photo stop in Mykonos and a must-see are the four Chora windmills that overlook the waterfront, the famous Venice Beach and the resident pelican, Pedro. At night the town is bustling and it is known for its many clubs and all-night parties especially on Paradise Beach. Not to be forgotten is the food; fresh seafood and succulent grilled meats accompanied with an authentic Greek salad are a must!

May 2006... Up until this point in my life, I had not visited Las Vegas. The opportunity came by way of an invitation to join my friend Juli as she attended a conference in "Sin City."

We arrived at the airport and took a taxi over to the MGM Grand Hotel. Immediately upon arrival in Las Vegas, I saw the similarities between the airport, hotels and the restaurants, to that of the cruise ship experience, except on a much larger scale. Instead of entertaining thousands of people as we do onboard, in

Las Vegas they cater to tens of thousands of visitors at any given time. Surprisingly the city runs like clockwork just like a cruise ship. From arrivals to departures, efficiency, cleanliness, and friendliness, right down to the polite sanitation personnel on the street greeting me with an energetic "Good morning" along with a great big smile.

On our second day in town, I walked the entire Vegas strip. I was just as excited as a kid at Disneyland would be. For me this was a big kid's amusement park, I stopped at every single sight along the way hoping not to miss a thing. I found the architecture and interior design of the hotels akin to living in a make-believe world. Although I had seen Vegas in pictures and in movies, it was all grander than anything I could have imagined. The Venetian reminded me of Venice, walking inside you could believe that you really were in Venice, complete with canals, music, gondola rides and gondoliers. Juli and I dined at the Bellagio with front row seats overlooking the famous water fountain shows, notwithstanding a little mist it was quite an aquatic display of lights and music. All of the restaurants and food experiences exceeded my expectations, as did the two shows I attended, Cirque de Soleil and Mama Mia.

Following our two-day vacation in Vegas, we travelled to St. George, Utah, to visit Juli's parents. We drove from Nevada to Utah and along the way we experienced the beauty of the American Midwest. The red, orange and white colours in the rock formations spanning as far as the eye could see changed hourly as the sun repositioned from east to west. I could not have imagined such breathtaking and incredibly peaceful scenery from the highway, each and every turn in the road was no less sensational and dramatic than the last.

We decided to extend our visit to Nevada to enjoy the peace and tranquility, rather than return to Vegas as originally planned. We enjoyed sightseeing through Bryce Canyon with its crimson-coloured hoodoos, which are spire-shaped rock formations, and

Zion National Park with its unique array of plants and vegetation. At every view and at every turn, the landscape was more breathtaking than the last.

I am fortunate to have travelled frequently to some beautiful and exotic destinations through work or personal travel. Occasionally throughout my life, I had feared that I had seen so much that nothing in the future was going to impress me, and yet it just keeps happening over and over and over again! Our world is comprised of extraordinary sights to see and exceptional experiences to be had!

Another great perk which I fortunately was offered while working for the cruise line was discounted cruise offers, which I had taken advantage of on a few occasions. One particular vacation I took was with Janice to the Caribbean. Janice had never cruised before and what better opportunity to accompany my friend and show her how cruising is done. At the completion of one of my contracts, I disembarked the ship in San Juan, Puerto Rico and met up with Janice who had flown down.

We spent the afternoon exploring this colourful and beautiful old town with its steep narrow streets made of blue cobblestone. The streets are lined with picturesque colonial buildings in various pastel colours that date back to the 16th and 17th century. The area is surrounded by a massive stone wall, which acts as the city's first defense. We took time to wander through the small shops, and it did not matter where you were you could hear the local music coming from various directions. San Juan is one of my much-loved places to explore; it is also another favourite food destination of mine. After hours of walking and blistered feet, I took Janice to my preferred Puerto Rican restaurant, the Parrot Club, and indulged in some delicious local cuisine while breathing in the historical Spanish charm of the island. We spent the night in a quaint little hotel and the following day we boarded one of our sister ships for two back-to-back seven-night Caribbean Cruises.

October 2007... Another memorable vacation was with my mom; it was a 14-night round trip to Hawaii out of Los Angeles. Prior to the cruise, we spent five days in California visiting another friend of mine, Valerie. We toured Hollywood and the film studios and peered through the windows of fashionable stores on Rodeo Drive. We walked along the beaches in Malibu, choosing which of the many extraordinary homes along the coast we would buy if we could. Dreaming truly is a wonderful thing! We stopped to have lunch on the waterfront, drove along the California coast and ended our lovely day by watching an extraordinary sunset while strolling along the Santa Monica Pier. Our cruise to Hawaii was marvellous; we made four stops in Hawaii including, Hilo, Kailua Kona, Lahaina (Maui), and Honolulu (Oahu). This was another vacation in paradise; a stress-free way to island-hop while enjoying five-star service.

In May of that year, I vacationed with Juli once again; she invited me to join her on a luxury cruise ship sailing through the Caribbean. It was definitely another vacation opportunity of a lifetime. We cruised for eight days to Honduras, Guatemala, and Cozumel where in addition to the glorious sand and sea we enjoyed fantastic meals, shows, and amenities, including a marble bathroom and walk-in closet in our suite. Unfortunately, and I chuckle as I say this, we were unable to use our veranda as it was too hot. Ah well, if that was the worst of our problems – life is good!

Spirit ...

～ele～

May 2005... In December of 2004 Dad was diagnosed with colon and spinal cancer and given six to nine months to live. Dad passed away almost six months to the day. It was his departure that I believe was the catalyst to making my first conscious step on my spiritual path.

I was fortunate that I had been home for a two-month vacation. However, three weeks prior to my leaving the nurse was at our home for her routine visit and after examining dad, she said, "It doesn't look like he will be with us for much longer, at most maybe a few more weeks." Based on that information I informed the office that I might have to delay my return if my dad were to pass before I was scheduled to leave. As it turned out, Dad hung in there. When I left home to return to work I hugged him and said good-bye. I could feel it deep down; I knew that I was not going to see him again. I even went so far as to put my bags in the taxi and ran back into the house for one more hug and one last farewell.

I flew into Nice to catch the ship in Villefranche the following morning. While there I took full advantage of my quality alone time in France. It was a beautiful day, cool with a slight breeze. My hotel was on the edge of town across the street from the waterfront and stunning boardwalk; it was about 2 pm by the time I settled in. I decided to walk along the harbour front, which was the perfect scenario to relax, breathe in fresh sea air while reflecting on the past two months at home with my dad. Although very challenging, as Dad was very ill, I could not believe that I was so fortunate to have had my vacation at that exact moment and thus the quality time we spent together. I recalled all the in-depth conversations we had, all the laughter and the tears right up to the moment of our heartfelt goodbye! I strolled along the boardwalk all the way to the other end of town and back. I returned just in time for a late dinner at the hotel before a well-needed good night's sleep to prepare for the upcoming contract.

The following day, on the evening of my arrival on board, I had just finished my first shift and was in my cabin when the phone rang, it was Mom, and she asked me, "Are you sitting down?" My heart stopped and I knew at that instant, Dad had left us. I noted later that evening that my watch had stopped at 3:30 pm my time which, with the time difference, was the exact time back home of Dad's passing. The following morning, my watch began working again. People say that a loved one does not leave you; that they are with you and that they watch over you once they have moved on. I never paid any attention to this or acknowledged this thought until my dad passed. It was shortly thereafter that I knew it was, in fact, true. His presence was felt immediately after his departure and interestingly it was a pleasant, peaceful and calming experience.

I chose not to go home; I had decided before Dad passed that I would prefer to mourn on my own rather than being comforted and hearing tales from those I rarely saw when he was alive. In addition, I knew that Mom was in good hands with family and friends and all the necessary arrangements had been made prior to my leaving. I was well supported; Giannis was onboard, as was another very close friend who had met Mom and Dad, so I had all the comfort I needed. Everyone was amazing and the possibility for me to leave to go home was available. I spoke with Mom daily, and deep down I knew that I did what was right for me and

I have never regretted my personal decision to stay onboard, nor did Mom.

My sales desk was off to the left-hand side in the Grand Foyer, and Miguel, the Concierge, a close friend, had his desk just across from mine. We were so close we could and would overhear each other's conversations with the guests. Miguel received a call from home a few days after my dad passed; his father had passed away. Miguel flew home to be with family and returned a week later. The morning after Miguel's return, an irate guest was intently going off on him. I don't remember exactly what it was, but I do know that it wasn't that serious and definitely didn't warrant the rude behaviour. As Miguel faced me from behind his desk, and I faced him from behind the guest, at that exact moment during the episode we both looked up and locked eyes. Absolutely no words were needed, we could feel each other's energy and what we both were thinking simultaneously was, *"We both just lost our fathers and are not in a position to discuss it, and you are upset about, what?"* That was a very interesting experience and one that I will never forget. Miguel and I have talked about that day often. What really stuck out in our minds is that we do not know what may be transpiring in someone's life or how they may be feeling. We never really know what is going on with the individual who is in front of us. Accordingly, nobody deserves to be treated badly under any circumstance.

> *If we were to lay our problems out for all to see,*
> *we would realize that we all have problems of which*
> *many are the same.*

Seven months later I was sitting at my desk when I glanced over to my left at a frail old woman, she was wrapped in a blanket and sitting in a wheelchair. She was the mother of the gentleman that I was assisting with booking his next cruise. She was about seven feet away and I remember the lobby that evening as being quiet and dimly lit. As I looked over at her I saw a woman's face that eerily resembled my dad's, her demeanour – features, expression, body weight, and ailing frame were all too familiar but it was her eyes that looked up at me. The hair on my arms stood up and the strong emotions immediately crept up from the pit of my stomach, quickly rose through me and ended up as a lump in my throat. She was reminiscent of my dad in his last days, as he sat in his wheelchair. At that moment, I did not think it possible and yet it was so real, I was looking at this silhouette of the old woman yet I was clearly seeing and feeling the presence of my dad. As I held back the tears I remember thinking wow, and that on Christmas Eve!

Home ...

Despite being out at sea and travelling to exotic destinations, I have always secretly longed for a home; a little fixer-upper to become a safe refuge from the storms. Considering I was away for months at a time and a single income person, I felt that this dream was unattainable. I also have a hidden passion for decorating and design. I realize that the retelling of my story involves my life on a cruise ship and the places I have been to, so why include a section called "home?" The answer is; my house is my love, my dream come true, an achievement and most of all, my safe haven, and my happy place.

As I transitioned from banking to the cruise industry, I lived with my then recently divorced uncle in his house. It was a perfect arrangement that allowed me to move all my belongings, my car and my cat included to his place, while I travelled. I stayed for 10 years and I learned to appreciate living in a house. My first newly found adoration was a garden. What I loved most was how I felt knowing that I could wake up, pour myself a cup of coffee and drink it in the garden. With no prior experience or knowledge of gardening, I started puttering around in the flowerbeds and decided that I loved it. I did not know the difference between one flower and the next but I knew that I was enjoying everything to do with gardening; the trial and error – is it a weed or plant and the learning process – what exactly is manure made of? A big draw for me is the peace and quiet, being outdoors, and seeing the fruit of my labour; beautiful plants and flowers everywhere. As much as I love gardening, to this day I still am not very good at distinguishing a flower from a weed – now affectionately referred to as wildflowers, but what I do know is that my puttering around is very gratifying.

After 10 years my uncle retired and decided to move out to the country. As the universe would have it, the opportunity arose for me to purchase my own home and I jumped at the chance. It was a beautiful quaint little house, which required a lot of TLC, but it was mine.

The first project was to complete the transformation of the basement apartment. I wanted a space of my own because my mom and nephew would be living on the upper level. The apartment had a kitchen, a newly renovated bathroom and lots of potential. With a fresh coat of paint, I was ready to call it home. I was so excited to be a homeowner.

The next job was one I did not expect; I learned that there is more to owning a home than decorating. We had a major crack in the front porch, causing a small river to flow through the cold storage room and then into the basement. I decided not only would I have the crack repaired, I would replace the walkway down to the street with grass and create a garden wall. After it was completed I had a beautiful stone front porch, walkway, and a rock garden, which I designed. This was quite a financial undertaking and I then realized that I needed a landscaper, which was on the 63rd page of my to-do list! I tapped in on the skills I learned from puttering around in my uncle's garden; I'm now the landscaper and for almost free. Once the cold storage room was repaired and painted a beautiful Mediterranean yellow it became a wine cellar and houses beautiful wooden crates and racks which hold 130 bottles of homemade wines. Now that I have my wine cellar and I am no longer a wino, I am a wine connoisseur, with a good sense of humour.

About a year later, after dad's passing and my nephew's moving on, Mom and I decided to refresh the main floor; freshly painted mocha cream walls and white ceilings, trims, and doors complete the look and it is stunning. The next job was the back deck and fences, which desperately needed replacing. I designed a picture-frame neutral deck and fences with a cedar-colour trim; voilà another dream come true.

The hardwood floors were a disaster but despite being high on the priority list, they had to wait. During this time I was looking for furniture to complete the transformation. I had accumulated pieces of furniture, art, knick-knacks and clothing over the years, but as I looked over my "stash" after being away from home for more than a decade, I realized that I really wanted everything to be new in my new home. I was sorting through some clothing with Janice and we laughed as we reminisced over the past fashions that I was still hanging on to; full-length dresses with bold floral patterns and stripes and polka dots in bright red, yellow and pink. She was helping me decide what clothes to keep and what to throw away, it was agreed that I would keep 10 articles. Who would think this would be such a difficult process. It was just another example of getting emotionally attached to things, which we eventually really do need to part with.

A year later I eventually found the right furniture and we redid the main floor giving me "my dream home." Over the years I also had to endure what I like to call painful expenditures such as a new roof, new doors, weeping tiles etc. but all in all, looking back, I am absolutely thrilled with my little house adventures. Now, years later, when I am not travelling around the world, I am still fulfilling living my dream of enjoying my home and garden with my family and friends.

Amazement ...

ele

Once again I was thinking about how I go through life sort of like Forrest Gump, following my heart, taking one step at a time, and living in the moment. I am amazed how everything in my life just seems to miraculously flow and somehow the kinks get worked out along the way. Travelling can be stressful to most; from finding the ideal vacation, booking flights and hotels, dealing with luggage, check-in and immigration, unexpected costs to organizing, negotiating and arranging ground transportation in unfamiliar places. I realize that my career granted me the luxury of having my arrangements made, the itinerary was drawn up, almost all of my travel expenses were covered and I got to fly all over the world.

I shake my head at the sheer magnitude of it all, and the fact that it truly was all real! Once again, I count my blessings; for all that I have and all that I have experienced in my life.

Live life with an attitude of Gratitude!

I have been in hundreds of airports, hotels, and restaurants all over the world. I have walked the streets of foreign cities; entered into establishments and conversed with people even when I don't speak their language. I enjoy taking everything in while not knowing or caring what lies around the next corner; this to me is living! Not only that but I find that with this attitude, I am not often disappointed in whatever I find in the land of the unknown.

Even if by chance I may be disappointed, that is okay too. Even when things are not perfect in life, if you take a good look, you can always find a reason to appreciate something.

If there were no clouds or no rain,
we would not appreciate a sunny day.

Addictions ...

ele

I have been a smoker for the greater part of my life. I attempted to quit numerous times and did on two occasions; once for two years and the second time for seven months. I knew based on my family history that I had to quit. Our family history includes cancer, strokes and heart attacks, which made every doctor I saw, tell me to quit and quit now! In my mind I knew smoking was absurd; "Why am I still smoking?" I asked myself. Dad was 68 when he lost his battle with cancer, he had smoked all his life; he had also had several strokes which were warning signs. Though I had previously quit, the thought of attempting to quit a third time was just as fearful as quitting for the first time.

One afternoon, while attending to a guest at my desk, I let out a little cough. She apparently was concerned and ever so politely asked me, "Do you smoke?" My response was "Yes, unfortunately," to which she slowly leaned forward, gently touched my hand and ever so kindly with her southern accent, said, "Darling you really must quit." She was not the first person to tell me this. Interestingly, I took her statement to heart and today I believe that she was an angel sent to give me a very serious message. I did not immediately quit, however, her words never left me and I kept her kind gentle suggestion very close to my heart.

I received another sign and it made me realize that it was not the first one. I had for many years been experiencing circulation problems; I had numbness in both my arms and legs that would come and go. Years later, I began having issues with my throat. I began coughing, experiencing throat pain and on occasion shortness of breath, again, symptoms that would surface periodically and then pass. Eventually, the throat problems became worse and I could not ignore them, or wish them away; these flare-ups really caught my attention. My job entailed speaking to people all day at my desk, around the ship, and giving presentations on stage regularly. I was experiencing a scratchy throat, which worsened to the point that I had to have a bottle of water by my side and at times I needed to stop talking and take a drink before I could continue. It was then that I opened my eyes and truly paid attention to the signs. "Did I want to die young or prolong my life on a respirator, no?" I had finally tuned in to the fact that I had a very serious problem. I knew there was only one successful option. I knew exactly what I needed to do and I knew that the challenge ahead was not going to be easy.

Once again I decided that it was time to quit. I had gone three weeks without smoking and I thought that I would have been ecstatic, but for some reason, I was not. In all my attempts to quit smoking, this was the first time I had an understanding of my addiction. I realized that every day of victory is just that, one day; tomorrow would be another day and I would have to face my addiction once again. I knew that I would never be free of my desire to smoke. I now felt motivated and empowered with the acknowledgement of both these realizations.

Two months later when I returned to work I began smoking again. I did not consider this a failed attempt; rather, I acknowledged that some challenges take time and effort to overcome.

What is it about conquering our issues?
Why do we make it so difficult for ourselves?

I persevered despite failing time and time again. It took me three more years and a few more failed attempts before I managed to quit permanently and I am glad I did because I am here today healthy, happy and writing my life story!

History ...

.𝓮𝓵𝓮

his·to·ry – *noun* - the whole series of past events
connected with someone or something

Growing up in Canada I never really had a sense of history and
sadly I recall having no interest in learning about it when I was in
school. I knew my parents grew up in the midst of WWII in the
Netherlands, Mom was the oldest of three girls, born in 1939 and
Dad was the oldest of six kids born in 1936 but I felt no connection in my youth. Nevertheless, travelling as a young adult, the
seed was planted. As I travelled and matured the seed took root, I
developed an interest and I began to understand the importance
of history.

It was one o'clock in the afternoon on a beautiful warm and
sunny June day in Amsterdam. Amsterdam was our embarkation
port for various cruises including Scandinavia and Russia, Norway
and the Arctic Circle and the British Isles. We would alternate
these cruises during the summer months giving me the opportunity to indulge in this wonderful part of the world for three full
seasons. I had the morning off and the luxury of not having to set
an alarm. I slept until nine am and then headed out to explore this
700-year old city, and yes, this is another on the list of my favourite
places in the world.

I remember sitting at an outdoor café, which was built on

one of approximately 1,500 old bridges that overlooked the canals and the spectacular beauty of this living museum. The Museum District houses the Van Gogh Museum, works by Rembrandt and Vermeer are at the Rijksmuseum and modern art can be found at the Stedelijk Museum. I enjoyed wandering the narrow cobblestone streets, especially the ones that ran alongside the multitude of canals in this "Venice of the North." The canals are filled with beautifully designed and crafted canal boats and a multitude of planters filled with colourful flowers line the streets. Cycling is a part of the city's charm, there are old bicycles everywhere – thousands of them and numerous bike paths traverse the city at every turn. There are beautifully shaped crooked buildings with gabled facades that hover over the narrow streets like the leaning tower of Pisa. Amsterdam presents a glimpse back into the legacies of the city's 17th-century Golden Age.

Mom has cruised with me numerous times and on one occasion she and I were out exploring on a glorious day in Amsterdam. We were admiring the canals, the boats and the abundance of stunning flowers everywhere when I jokingly said, "We could sell our house and get a canal house boat here in Amsterdam." We paused, looked at each other before she said "Would you believe that it was right around 50 years ago today that I moved to Canada" – Wow! We both agreed that despite how lovely Amsterdam truly is we both love our life in Toronto.

Our travels to the various ports in England, Ireland and Scotland allowed us to experience firsthand the UK's famous cold grey damp weather, once again a lesson in "If it doesn't rain it's a beautiful day." This itinerary was another historical storybook filled with an abundance of things to see and do. We visited the mystical castles of Edinburgh, and explored the beautiful old stone houses that are scattered throughout the highlands in and around Inverness, the happiest place in Scotland. We even attempted to spot Nessie, the mythical Loch Ness monster. When in Cork you can visit Blarney Castle and partake in the age-old ritual of hanging upside down and kissing the Blarney Stone, the legendary stone of Eloquence, found at the top of the tower. They claim that if you kiss the stone (upside down) you will never be lost for words. Another thrill is getting lost in the ambiance of Dublin or Belfast, enjoying the local Irish specialties while spending quality time with the charming Celtic speaking people.

Our 12-night Scandinavian cruise included the following ports of call: Warnemunde, Germany; Helsinki, Finland; Stockholm, Sweden; Copenhagen, Denmark; Tallinn, Estonia; and St. Petersburg, Russia. Every port on this itinerary was an absolute gem but I will say that the highlight was a day trip to Moscow, which was a thrill of a lifetime! The tour included return flights from St. Petersburg, a complete city tour of Moscow and photo stops at major attractions. We were treated to an authentic Russian lunch that consisted of the most amazing beef stroganoff, which we delightfully washed down with oh so smooth Russian vodka – straight up! When I was young Moscow was a place where only a few had the opportunity to visit; it seemed so very far away and just as far out of reach to most. At that point in my life, I never imagined that I would be standing in the middle of Red Square and have the opportunity to view the Royal Treasures at the Kremlin.

Our repositioning cruise, in this case, transitioning the ship from Northern Europe to the Mediterranean, took us to La Havre, France's second-largest seaport, located at the mouth of the River Seine. It is not only a stunning city on its own but is very close to Paris, Honfleur, the beautiful island of Mont Saint-Michel and the beaches of Normandy. Another moving moment in my life was standing on Omaha Beach on a crisp sunny day. It was difficult to fathom that on this beach the Allied troops landed to battle for the liberation of France. It was a very sullen moment strolling in silence amongst the rows upon rows of crosses at the American Cemetery and Memorial, which overlooked the cliffs just a short distance away. These moments left us breathless. Words cannot describe how steeped in history all these countries are in this extraordinary part of the world; from art, literature, music, fashion, culture and of course the not so distant wars.

Throughout my life, I have listened to the historical tales and accounts of the tragic past while not being able to comprehend the reality of it all. I was not able to understand the magnitude of wars when I was young and did not develop a global view. However, this excursion left me thinking and appreciating our history as humans.

Presence ...

While home on vacation, on Oprah's recommendation, I read Eckhart Tolle's, *A New Earth*. It is the fourth book in a series of self-help books. I found it to be a difficult read but was determined to get through it. This book was a mind-shifting experience for me. Up until that point, I lived like most with a mind that would not quit, thinking about everything and anything, simultaneously. In retrospect, I should have read *The Power of Now* first, which is the initial book in the series. After reading both *A New Earth and The Power of Now* I began learning how to live in the present, to just be, in the here and now. I learned being present allows us to consciously let go of the past and not worry about the future, even if only for a very short time – now that was powerful to me!

We are continually being traumatized by something that has already occurred, it is done and gone and therefore cannot be changed. And if we are not focused on something in the past then we are thinking about the future; a constant stream of repetitive thoughts in our heads. We become anxious about what we are going to do, what we should do or would like to do. We allow our fear of the future to take control. Allowing our minds to constantly chatter on about the past or the future robs us of the only thing we really do have and that is the present moment, right here and right now!

I needed to read both books a few more times for a new way of thinking to really sink in. However, the first read-through gave me the ability to tune into the possibilities; my curiosity was peaked and I started to look at life from a new and different perspective. I returned to work and as usual I got caught up in the shipboard routine; however, when returning this time, I noticed a difference in myself. For the first time in my life, even if it was only for a short period, I was able to consciously live in the present. I was focusing on what was happening right here and right now. Once you have the ability to be present you can then take a deep breath at any given moment and ask, "What is the next right move?" Then relax. The answer will always come. This is my screen saver.

Be completely in the present moment and ask...
What's the next right move?
...Then relax!

Reality ...

~elle~

This particular cruise was a charter for Soap Opera fans, which came complete with 35 Soap Opera stars. I was intrigued watching these famous people. I didn't know any of them because I was not a soap fan; nevertheless, it was fun to watch. No doubt, they were very good looking, dressed glamorously as to be expected and had an interesting group of excited and dedicated followers on their heels. We were chuckling and joking amongst ourselves saying that they, for a living, act out some of life's most outlandish stories and here we are actually living out some of those scenarios.

What struck me as interesting was their ability not to make eye contact, lest they draw you in for a conversation! It was clear that they had more; they had more material assets than most and some people would gladly trade places for some of that fame and glamour.

What a different life from the one I led. Nevertheless, at the end of the day, I realize that I too had an extraordinary life. I could choose to be ready to go out in 15 to 30 minutes, travel the world receiving no attention, and I didn't have to wear high heels every-where I went.

Just as some people are star-struck by actors; some were fascinated by my career choice. I recall when I told people that I worked on a cruise ship; it would instantly spark a very long conversation. When I was introduced, the conversation would begin with "This is Laura, she works on a cruise ship!" For all the years that I worked at the bank – nobody ever introduced me by saying, "This is Laura, she works at the bank." This would lead to a series of questions and me taking on the role of Ambassador of Travel! A Cruise Director once said when he is not on ships and someone asked what he did for a living his response would be, "I work in a shoe store." He said that it guaranteed a much shorter conversation. Do not get me wrong; throughout my entire career I was proud to tell people what I did for a living. I would very often say out loud, "I continually had to pinch myself because I could not believe that I was living the life that I was."

True to human nature, friends would continually ask me, "When are you going to give up this fantasy life and come back to reality?" People were shocked when I would tell them that I had been working onboard for so many years and most would ask me "Why?"

Many see ship life as confined; small spaces, many rules, long days and a transient life of sorts. I, on the other hand, have always felt like a bird, free to fly and explore not only the world but also life! I followed my heart, my inner voice and my dreams while experiencing this glorious planet of ours. Deep down I always knew that despite the peer pressure along the way, I was doing what was right for me. We all have our own unique stories of following our hearts, our dreams and finding our own reality.

Life is in how you live it
and I lived mine like a star, in my eyes!

Growth ...

. ℓℓ~

June 2009... It is unusual for me to feel loneliness, however on this particular contract, I was feeling just that. New ships were being added to the fleet, friends had moved on to other vessels and I knew very few people when I arrived on board. A part of working on ships is having to leave the comfort of our families and homes for months at a time. In the past when I returned to work I would be met by friends and people I knew. On this contract, I returned as a total stranger. I was taken aback by this odd new sensation of alienation whilst in the midst of so many people; this was a feeling I had not had for a very long time.

At the time I attributed my feelings to the changes that were taking place in my life and around me. The company was growing at a rapid rate and as a result, there were many changes on all levels of the business – new procedures, new rules and regulations, more demands and higher expectations. New ships were being added to meet the projected demands of travellers and therefore there were many new crewmembers to meet, train and get to know. Additionally, despite it being my 13th year at sea, I was about to embark the ship to face some unexpected personal challenges. Not long after arriving on board I realized that I was experiencing strong feelings for a crewmember. However, with his mixed messages he was definitely rattling my nerves and heightening some sensations that had not surfaced in me for quite some time.

One moment he would appear flirty and interested and the next, somewhat aloof, and this went on for most of the contract. In the end nothing happened and I was resigned to periodically seeing his beautiful smile which would brighten my day and I let the rest of the relationship play out in my mind! To top it off, a close friend of mine had seriously let me down by proving time and time again that life was all about her. Overall I was not feeling the love in my life that I normally felt. My situation became more challenging as I began to focus on how young the new crewmembers were getting and how the atmosphere onboard felt like junior high.

I did not have clarity at the time to see the lessons being presented. I was too busy blaming everything and everyone around me for all of my life's shortcomings. Today I can clearly see that all of the challenges I encountered were seeds planted only to grow into some of the lessons in my life. I didn't see it then but now I realize that my "love interest" was not right for me and that my "dear friend" for many reasons was not someone I wanted in my life. Looking back I believe that this period, although painful at the time, was a big step for my inner growth.

It was after enduring these situations and coming out on the other side, that I began to see that there is more to life than "What's in it for me."

Some of Gods greatest gifts are unanswered prayers – Garth Brooks

I do recall, despite the heartbreaks, deciding that I was not going to let my challenges get me down. I took advantage of my alone time; I went to the gym and caught up on some TV series. It was not long before I was back in the swing of things with some new friends. Another amazing fact about ship life is, when you do meet and get to know someone, it can feel as if you have known him or her for forever, all in just in a matter of weeks.

Wounds ...

I think one of my best qualities is my sense of humour. I make an effort to laugh whenever possible, because life is too short not to laugh. I have always said, "If we don't laugh, then the only alternative is to cry."

In addition to encountering challenges and stress, I, just like you, also encounter various fears and insecurity issues that cause sadness and pain. Pain not only causes suffering, but suffering of any kind is an absolute waste of the short valuable time we have on this earth.

Can we go through life without pain and sadness? Of course not, we all from time to time come up against things in life that hurt us but there is a secret to eliminating suffering and stress; we must face the pain or sadness and be totally present in the situation. We must not think of the current circumstance in terms of the past or future, we must just think of it in this exact moment in time and face it head-on. Instead of asking ourselves "What can I do right now this second?" we tend to replay what we have already been through. It's not the situation, which causes us to feel pain, *it's how we respond to it!* The past cannot be changed so we need to release any guilt about what has been done or how it was perceived. We are in the here and now. Realize that in this moment a life's lesson can be learned.

Accept the present; this is where you are – face the storm head-on!

When I am faced with challenges I recall one of my favourite Tony Robbins lines, *"What's great about this?"* Initially, my answer was "Nothing; nothing is great about this or the way I am feeling." However, Tony instructs in his coaching that if this is our answer we are to ask again, and again, and once again – until we receive a different answer. Sometimes it does take some time and effort but there is always a positive answer. It can and will be found if we ask the right questions. The answer may not rectify the situation, nevertheless, it will make us feel a little bit better and help anchor us in the present moment, making the situation easier to deal with.

Once you have reached that calm in-the-moment feeling, you will need to find a release. I believe having a good sense of humour often elevates the mood. Then we begin to move forward one small step at a time, not allowing our minds to take us to the past or the future, but rather staying in the present.

We may not laugh about this now but someday, somehow, we will.

If we can adopt this attitude, even if we do not initially laugh, we will look back with at least a half-smile.

Mystery ...

ele

I remember the weather that day, it was cool and grey, but inside was filled with the glorious aroma of turkey stuffing and a 12-hour love story marathon was on TV, life was good!

Once again I was home on vacation. This past contract had been for four months and I had been working in the same position now for eight years. I felt as if my life was stagnant, just a daily routine with nothing exciting happening; I had become complacent. Prior to leaving I had a chance to meet and chat with my replacement, Randi. It was in that conversation with a stranger that I came to the realization of how full and rich my life truly was. I never held back talking about how I love my life and how blessed I am; excellent performance appraisals, a secure job, travel and a circle of loving family and friends. Regardless of how blessed we think or know we are, we occasionally lose sight of our reality. Things in our lives become, or appear to become, the norm and mundane.

I realized I had been doing the same thing for quite some time. What I really needed and wanted were some new personal challenges and uplifting experiences in my life; that was the turmoil I was feeling deep down inside of me.

While at home relaxing, I was able to spend time contemplating about my life. I recognized that although my life was wonderful, I knew I still wanted more. I also acknowledged that I had absolutely no idea what the more was. However, just the wanting of something was a good thing as it meant that I was looking to expand and grow. My major concern was, exactly what is it I want and that was a mystery. A passage from Tony Robbins reads, "*If you're not getting the right answers – you may be asking the wrong questions!*" This made me realize that it was time for me to reassess my questions. That combined with a little mystery in life really was not a bad thing!

**If we are not getting the right answers,
then we are asking the wrong questions!**

Fifty ...

I awoke to another beautiful sunny day in St. Maarten. I love St. Maarten! Immediately after opening my eyes and before getting up, my first thought was *OMG I am 50 today!* I remember taking a trip back in my mind, visualizing turning 30 and I remember feeling devastated; however, I did get over it relatively quickly when I realized that nothing really changed except for the number. I wasn't bothered by age when I turned 40, by then I had figured out that we are only as young or as old as we feel. Upon turning 50, I never dreamed I would be where I was in life or feel that good at that age.

I started to think about where exactly I was in my life compared to where I thought I would be. I took stock; I was 50 and single, never married, an ex-banker, who was travelling around the world visiting exotic places that most can only dream of. I was in great health and financially secure. Although like everyone else I had no idea what tomorrow was going to bring, nevertheless I was pleased with how my life had turned out so far. I knew that I was living a life that was unconventional to most, but again I knew that I was doing what was right for me.

I jumped out of bed with a surprising amount of energy, kind of like when you open your eyes and know you have a plane to catch. I had the morning and afternoon off, Tammy had a special trip planned for us and I didn't have a clue what this mystery trip entailed. What I did know was that any outing with Tammy was sure to be an extraordinary adventure. We left the ship; it was a perfect warm sunny day with clear blue skies and just the warmth of the sun on our skin felt amazing after being in the air conditioning on the ship. We walked to the end of the pier and started our day off by stopping at a small local beverage stand where Tammy ordered us two of their Caribbean Specials consisting of rum, coconut, and a few other local special ingredients; not a bad breakfast! After enjoying our breakfast beverages, we took a taxi over to the other side of the island where we caught a small boat, over to a smaller island. There we found ourselves some beach chairs, chilled, had a swim and caught some sun before we headed over to a tiny local waterfront restaurant to enjoy my birthday lunch. I have never been one to plan major festivities for my birthdays, but this was the big 5-0 and here I was on a tiny island in the Caribbean with one of my dearest friends; this was in my opinion, the best possible way to celebrate. If all of this wasn't already enough, the highlight of this birthday adventure and another event beyond anything I could have imagined was that I got to go into the ocean to choose my very own lobster! Wow!

Single ...

︾e︾

Guests would routinely ask, "How can you live on ships for so long and what about your family or boyfriend?" My response was, "Not only do I have an amazing job; my bed is made for me, my towels are changed daily and my bathroom is cleaned regularly. Not to mention my food is prepared, my dishes get washed and as far as my laundry goes, I throw it on the bed and it comes back washed, pressed and on hangers. The bonus is, I travel the world and they pay me to do so. Am I really going to trade all that in for a man?"

I started this book by saying "If I had been told at 20 that I would be 50 and never been married..." I, like most women growing up in the 60s and 70s, thought that I would meet Mr. Right, have my two-point-two kids, a dog, and a white picket fence. However, as some of us grow older and mature we begin experiencing life on our own terms and our opinions and outlook on life changes. Why? Because once we have found our career, have our own place, our cat and our car, we have independence and our own voice and that is not only a beautiful thing, it is powerful. Does that mean we have found total happiness? Of course not! Does that mean we should all be single? Of course not!

I have wonderful memories of my life before my career on ships. I had great friends and a lovely place to live. My home was always clean, I could enjoy a peaceful cup of coffee in the morning, listen to the music of my preference, savour meals of my choosing and never having to watch sports or disagree with anyone. My cat was always meowing before I could even put my key in the door and she loved being by my side. I had enough funds to do what I chose to do, go where I decided to go and buy what I wanted, again with no reason to battle. Not too shabby for someone who has been single throughout her life.

Another one of the most frequently asked questions was, "Why have you never married?" I have two answers. The first one is, "Because I am having too much fun in this life, maybe in my next one." The second is, "I haven't slowed down enough for anyone to catch me." I occasionally ask myself, why have I not met my Mr. Right? At this point in my life, I know exactly why. I have chosen to focus on what I want. I wanted to work on cruise ships and I now look back and realize that seeing and experiencing the world had for a very long time been and still is one of my greatest desires in life.

When I look back, I see that except for my relationship with Giannis, which at the time fit into my lifestyle, a relationship with someone on land prior to my ship career would have taken me away from the life I truly desired and I do believe that everything in life happens (or doesn't happen) for a reason. That's not to say that I didn't have fun trying but as far as my *Mr. Right*, he and I obviously weren't on the same ship at the same time; if he was, I somehow missed him!

Online dating seems to be the thing to do in this day and age. I haven't tried it, I laugh when I think about what my ad would have said while I was out at sea … Away for four months, home for two, looking for a serious relationship. One day while I was on the treadmill, I was thinking, what I would put in an ad…

Ms. Right …

I've spent the first half of my life travelling and exploring half of this amazing world and my goal is to spend the second half discovering the rest. I have a great appreciation for all that this spectacular world has to offer and I love learning about all aspects of it.

Mr. Right…

Do you take fond memories and valued lessons from your past?
When you dream about the future; do you have an action plan in order to achieve your dreams?
Do you cherish every present moment and live life to the fullest?
Do you appreciate the sunset (or least pretend to for the sake of your partner)?
Do you love to kiss and snuggle?
Do you love to travel; to enjoy local cuisine and vintage while watching the world go by?

If you answered yes to all of the above, you may have found your Ms. Right.

Do I fear growing old and being alone? I do think about it but no, not at all. I really feel deep down that I will meet my soul mate someday. If by chance I do not, I will still have lived a satisfying life as I have truly found my place in this world as an independent, happy and content human being. I love to spend time with people just as much as I enjoy spending quality time alone. I can recall numerous times between relationships when I felt and was very lonely. When I think back on those times, I remember that they are just memories. As like most memories they can be confusing, however, if you sort through them properly – let go of the bad and hang onto the good, life can be extremely fulfilling, even when single!

Energy ...

If there is one thing that is very evident about me is that I cannot sit still; I am a bundle of energy. The joke was if I couldn't sit down with a drink and a smoke, I would never stop moving and doing. While at home on vacation, some shipmates came by for a visit. After some observation of our high spirits, Mom said, "Now I know what you all have in common, your friends are exactly like you – energy overdose!"

I had never really stopped to think about it but this is how we are on the ships, always on the run. In addition to our upbeat mood, we had to have physical energy to do what we did. We'd wake up, race off to work, run out to enjoy our short time off and then hustle back to report for duty. We'd finish a meal and be on the move again before the last mouthful of food was swallowed since we had to get back to work. At times, we would shower and change our clothes up to three times a day, for some maybe more. For some, a quick shower was a way to re-energize between shifts. Some of us were so wired at the end of the day that the only thing that would slow us down was a good work out, a bad movie, or a few drinks accompanied by friends for the day's debriefing.

Although there is a routine, there is no routine; this leads to a high energy on your toes state. On ships, we never know what is going to happen next and things do not always go as planned. Various circumstances cause rescheduling, reorganizing and adjustments to happen on a continuous basis. Employee work schedules and events around the ship change regularly due to a multitude of different reasons and all of those changes cause other changes, and accordingly, we are always busy living in the moment and flexibility and adaptability are mandatory requirements to work onboard.

Paradise ...

⸎

On this particular cruise, we were hosting a Jazz Charter and my Cruise Sales services were not required, so I was off duty for the entire cruise. The game plan for the first port of call was lunch in Key West. I slept in, woke at 10:30, showered, had coffee and did my nails. Tom called at 11:15 to say that he was just about ready to go. At 11:30 we were on the road. After a little shopping we had a splendid lunch on a patio on Duval Street. It was a beautifully clear and mild day; Key West was encountering a cool spell, however, it was nothing compared to the horrific winter storms that were occurring in the north-eastern US. It was such a lovely day that we decided not to return the ship immediately.

We stopped at a waterfront watering hole and indulged in the daily umbrella-in-a-glass special. As we were sipping our drinks and soaking up the atmosphere, I asked Tom, "If you were at home right now during the snowstorm, where would you be dreaming of being?" The answer was clear to both of us – right here at this exact moment in time, on this pier surrounded by blue waters. The temperature was perfect; the breeze refreshing, the skies were blue and the sun was shining. We were in a postcard picture; feet up, drinks in hand and off in the distance was a small island covered in palm trees and sand-coloured homes nestled in the groves as our backdrop. This truly was a paradise for us and home to some very lucky people.

It was time to leave our place in paradise to return on board. We finished off the day with dinner, caught Bruce Springsteen's Super Bowl halftime performance, and then settled in for a night of Acoustic Alchemy in the theater. It was a wonderful evening and an end to a perfect day.

Ageless ...

I began my career on the cruise ships in my mid-30s, a time when most are settled with a career and family. Most applicants for this line of work are in their early 20s, full of life and energy. I found that it did not matter your age or energy level, cruise ship life does keep you young at heart. I have always felt as young as those around me. There is no talk about aches and pains; instead, the conversations are always about what is current. One of these conversations happened when referring to a love interest a crewmember said, "Oh my, he's 10 years younger than me!" This comment came from a 30-year-old. I laughed and said, "Everyone is 10 years younger than me, at least." I talked about how unfair it is that for every year I get older the new crew gets younger so in reality the age gap really broadens with each passing year. It happens on land too but I think due to the large number of employees and continuous turnover, it is amplified on ships.

After that conversation, I realized that it is not youth lost but rather a progression from youth to maturity. Conversely, why should we be envious of someone young? Age is not a competition; aging should be celebrated as the collection of memories for different periods in your life. Therefore, we could ask ourselves, "Why would we be envious of where they are, we have already been there so in actuality they should be envious of us for our experience and wisdom and not us of them for what was once upon a time for us."

Throughout these discussions about age, I was left with a very interesting nugget. At that particular moment, I was 48 years old and living a life which most would never have the opportunity to experience. I became aware of how much youth I had in my life at that time. I can honestly say that even though I have loved all the stages of my life I am still living and feeling as terrific today as I did back then.

Correspondence ...

There is something to be said about putting pen to paper to detail your thoughts, describe an event, place or experience. Before emails, text, Instagram or Facebook became the media of communication there was the hard copy letter. It was not so long ago that you had to purchase tools to compose a letter; you needed a pen, paper, envelope, stamp and a mailbox or post office, a lot just to say, "Hi!" Writing a letter was time-consuming and made it challenging to stay in touch. Although unread for almost two decades, I still have all the letters from family and friends.

Following is an actual old-fashioned letter composed and sent to my family and friends back home very shortly after the birth of email.

My Adventures in Norway ☺

Hello all,

I have been trying to send an update for the past two weeks but it's been impossible so tonight, although exhausted from a long day, I have put my PJ's on, I will at least start to write you all from my room.

Last year I left Norway after completing two cruises saying, "It's nice." That was due to the weather; all I recall is it being very cold and some nice fjords. I didn't venture out as often last season; the itinerary this year did change for the better, which made a difference as well.

I proved my own saying to be true "travel with no expectations and you can only be pleasantly surprised." I told Mom before I left that I was not overly excited about returning to work and this contract – once again, having no expectations, I was blown away; it was spectacular!!!

I'll start where I left off in my last email debriefing after that bitterly cold day in Honningsvag; it was like we sailed off to the Med. The weather since has, for the most part, been amazing!!

Our next stop was Molde where Tammy and I attempted to climb to the top of the mountain right off the edge of town, which was a 10-minute walk from the ship. Tammy is the new Shore Excursions Manager, she replaced Charlotte who has gone home for vacation – I love this woman! I was wearing white jeans and a shirt and after about an hour of hiking up I melted, it was so warm. The views of the town, the mountain's and lakes were stunning and well worth the effort.

The following day we were in Geiranger, Norway. This is definitely one of the most spectacular places I have ever been too. We drove up the mountain in a minivan for about fifteen minutes, got dropped off. We hiked up two kilometers and then down about six back into town, where we found a patio watering hole and stopped to reward ourselves with a tasty beverage. Once onboard we had a sail away party for our loyalty club members – during which we celebrated the fourth of July with champagne and a breathtaking sail away through the very narrow fjords, with a grand performance by the seven sisters waterfalls, which towered above us along the way. I took about 100 photos today and as we hiked we passed through herds of goats and sang hiking songs like "sound of music." Unbelievable day!

Next port of call was Olden – another incredibly scenic spot. I took a crew tour – a 45-minute bus ride and then another 45-minute hike up to the glacier and then back down again.

The final stop for the cruise was Bergen. What an amazingly beautiful city surrounded by mountains and fjords. It was a cool but sunny day, we strolled the city streets, through Bryggen (the colourful wooden houses and shops on the old wharf), and then over to the waterfront market, and enjoyed, in addition to the ambiance of it all, a fresh smoked salmon sandwich.

Back in Amsterdam, our turn around port, we ran out to do some shopping and then to a patio for lunch. We had just arrived at the restaurant and it started to pour so we put up the umbrella, lit the candle on the table and enjoyed, once again, smoked salmon for lunch and a glass of wine. As the world was scrambling for cover - our experience – once again was awesome! By the time we finished our meal the rain was gone.

Our first stop on this cruise was Alesund. It was a cool, grey, partially rainy day. I had gone to the gym and taken a nap, as I had been here a few times. Arctic Circle day, weather was glorious. In Tromso, the weather was overcast and cool and it was Sunday, so I went to the gym and then to the spa – got my hair cut and highlighted – light copper streaks – looks amazing.

Back to Honningsvag, where we did the crab safari last

cruise in our, what I referred to as, moon suits – bright red, full-body thermal wear – as we were travelling in a speedboat in sub-zero temperatures, searching for crabs. OK, the crabs were already in a trap, ready for us to load onto our boat, take them to another location, where they were cooked in massive pots of boiling water in a larger than life tent. Nevertheless – it was an awesome experience and we ate crabs that were larger than any I had ever seen in my entire life! This week the weather was fabulous! We have not seen much sunshine or temps above zero in this port, however today we had clear blue skies and would you believe it was twenty-two degrees Celsius!

I called Tammy at about 9:30 and she said, "Come on tour with us at 10:30!" I told her that I had to work till 11 but that I would see what I could do. At ten I called the Hotel Director and said "I have never seen weather like this here, all is in order, could I possibly leave early to go on tour?" to which he replied, "sure, enjoy." So off I went. It was chaos on the pier – everyone wanting to get on the buses to the North Cape – the most northerly point in Europe, due to the incredible weather, so we were not able to get on a tour bus. Too bad for us; instead the shore side excursion agent drove us in a small van, stopping at various points that the tours went to as well as special photo stops along the way… Life is good! We went to see a local artist, met her personally and received one of her works of art. I picked it out, went to pay her and she said "a gift for a special visitor." We went to a small village to the Christmas house and had local cake and beverage (glug – warm fruit juice with nut flavouring). We arrived at the North Cape – clear blue skies, warm and you could see for miles. It was incredible and so was the movie we saw about the North Cape and Northern lights. We arrived *back at the ship around two pm, went upstairs for pizza, checked my work emails, took a short nap and then back to work for the evening. If you think that is enough excitement for one day, nope – guess what we had for dinner? Fresh caught King crab legs, as the tour operator gave Tammy a huge bag, which we enjoyed with Tammy's special South African mayonnaise and chilli concoction. We also received seagull eggs – a Norwegian delicacy (they're twice the size of regular eggs, the shell is blue with brown spots, the egg white is sort of transparent with an orange yolk). We ate them warm, just cooked, with salt and butter. What an amazing meal! After dinner, I ended this wonderful day enjoying a glass of wine up in the observation lounge with Arnie, our Norwegian specialist onboard and a wonderful man who was always a delight to talk too. He too was writing a book of his life; he's travelled all over the world on ships, is married and a grandfather – sixty-five and so incredibly full of life. Now he lectures part-time when he wants to.*

As I was saying goodnight to him in front of the guest elevators – he gave me the typical European kiss on each cheek - a gentleman came up to us and said, "oh so the crew kisses the guests these days." I replied by saying, "I normally always have a response but this time you've got me. It was so funny, we all laughed. I also told him "see - no secrets on a cruise ship."

Molde – today I went on another tour with the shore x staff. The port agent picked us up in a minivan and we drove out to see WW2 barracks and then sat out on a patio and ate pancakes with butter and sugar, and a coffee. Funny note… on tour the guests spend an hour visiting the barracks and then 20 minutes for the coffee break – we did the opposite – 20 minutes, including a short WW2 movie and then an hour out on the deck enjoying the treats and the glorious sunshine. A deer even came out to visit us. On the way to the barracks, we stopped at a small fishing village & met another local artist. She had a big beautiful cat, which I, of course, wanted to take back to the ship. We then went to the agent's house to let her dogs out (more like black bears as they were about the same size as me) and then we all took a 10-minute hike behind the house through the woods, which lead us to the waterfront. It was rocky, similar to northern Ontario. It was stunning! Then we took the van to the area's best-kept secret – beautiful beachfront (it was the only beach that I had seen in Norway). We then took a drive along the famous Atlantic road and then back to the ship.

Then next port day I did a full-day tour with the guests in Geiranger. Once again, it was spectacular and definitely the highlight of Norway! The weather, for the most part, was warm and sunny until we got up to the very top of the mountain and all you could see was fog and it was raining. I said to the agent "is this a bad joke?" It did clear briefly and you could see the famous picture of the fjord and the ship, way down below. I ran back to the bus to tell the guests. We did stop again further down the mountains and did get photo ops. I worked for a few hours and then went up to the crew spa night and had a wonderful 1-hour forty-five-minute hand and foot massage & French manicure.

My final Norway outing …Olden… Tammy said, "let's go out for a walk." We did and then she suggested going to get some snacks from the grocery store and go sit by the waterfront. That we did – got some flavoured mineral waters and some crunchy covered nuts and we just sat by the waterfront for an hour and a half taking in the fresh air, sunshine and peace and quiet (as you could only hear the birds and an occasional *voice from someone passing by). We drank in the glorious scenery, mountains which stretched in every direction and appreciated another glorious day in our life.*

Bergen – Unfortunately we had rain so I had lunch and went to the gym. I've been doing great as far as working out goes this contract.

Our Norwegian season was coming to a close and therefore so was Tammy & Arnie's visit with us. The Hotel Director invited them to dine in the Specialty Restaurant; I too was invited. We had an incredible evening, the food, service, wine, and company – outstanding! I had my usual favourite – Smoked Salmon and Peekytoe Crab Parfait appetizer that consisted of a layer of smoked salmon, avocado mousse, crabmeat & caviar topped with crème fraiche on a brioche. The main course was served with white gloves, on the plates with silver domed covers, which were simultaneously put on the table and lids, removed by the waiters. The Acapella boys came to sing for us and the evening ended with the amazing cheese trolley with various scrumptious cheeses coupled with a detailed explanation of each type - awesome. Just when you think that life couldn't get any better, I was invited to dine again at the same venue the following night as our Onboard Marketing Manager invited Tammy as she was leaving for vacation and Charlotte who was returning. I really do have friends in the right places, and once again a none the less spectacular evening with the girls.

Regarding work … never a dull moment, another novel, so let me summarize…

My Hostess is pregnant and leaving a cruise early. Her replacement is scheduled to come on the same day, brand new, so he requires training. We are currently in the middle of a new loyalty program launch. So if you don't hear from me for a while, you'll know why – I'll be a little busy. This is my payback for the past two wonderful cruises – lol.

My love life … getting lots of attention, nobody I'm interested in, but never the less it's flattering and life is fun!

I think that is my life's update for now and enough said for this email. Can you believe that all of this, and this is the reader's digest version, is only one and a half cruises – about two and a half weeks? Wow!!

I truly hope that you are well and that all is good in your life. Despite how it looks, life is not all about me. Please drop me a line with your updates anytime. Mom, thanks for the one-liner on your travelling adventures – haha – just joking, as always looking forward to coming home and catching up on our lives over a nice meal & wine on the back deck. All are invited to join us. I really should do this more often (evening in my room – writing) Bedtime – Ciao for now and goodnight, LUV LAURA

Interaction ...

꒜

Greetings are commonplace on a cruise ship; good morning, good afternoon, good evening, hello, ciao and so on! Today acknowledging and greeting guests is mandatory and a part of the crew-member training. As for myself, I can remember as far back as the first day that I arrived on board; I would always smile and greet everyone I met. I am not sure if it was because of the vacation atmosphere or mindset, or was it because we were always smiling and quick to offer up salutations. Nevertheless, it was the norm on a cruise ship and it definitely heightens the energy level.

However, once I left the ship I was confronted with indifference. I recall having to spend an entire day at the Miami airport where I did not acknowledge any of the other travellers or staff and they did not acknowledge me; this was a strange feeling for me. Once I arrived home what I noticed, as a rule, was that people do not speak to each other, other than a selected few, or those who are working in the service industry. I am not sure if interactions in small towns have remained the same, which in some ways is what gives it that charm and inclusiveness. Nowadays in urban neighbourhoods many people barely know their neighbours unless they have been in the area for a while; by then you know who the other long-standing residents are and can say, hello or at least nod a greeting.

Today, I pride myself on being that "weird" lady in the

grocery store; sure, I will just strike up a conversation with you in the checkout lane! Some people may ask, "How do you do it, just begin talking to strangers?" Communication skills and openness, to a certain degree, are honed from working on cruise ships and one's personality. Onboard we interact in casual conversations with guests and crewmembers talking about the fun things of a cruise, our lives or our jobs. There are however challenging conversations to be had at times; upset guests, medical emergencies and even deaths onboard, or from loved ones back home. As well as the occasional crisis, such as ship mechanical failures; these types of interactions enable us to forge deep connections with people who enter our lives.

I have always had a vision, and have vocalized it numerous times; I would love to get onto the subway on a Monday morning and start talking to everyone "Good morning, how are you?" "How was your weekend?" "Love that necklace, beautiful shoes – where did you get them?" That is how life is on ships and I personally think it could and should be like that on land as well. Can you imagine if more people would converse with each other? Just picture if we all did this, envision that subway ride to work on Monday morning. Today I still ask myself "Why is it that we can not have the same interactions on land as we do on ships?"

Friendships ...

What makes a true friend? I believe a true friend is always their authentic self, an open book, they do not feel the need to prove themselves to me and they expect nothing less in return. With no façade, we can truly be at ease just being ourselves and this is a wonderful thing. If we are fortunate to have a few true friends in our lifetime, we are blessed.

Not only do I have quite a number of friends around the globe, but I am also blessed because they are all truly amazing people. I realize that this is rare and something to be treasured. My experience has taught me that friends made during ship life come and go, however those we cherish will return somewhere somehow. Twenty years ago regular communication was "challenging," but today with email and social media, it truly is a small world after all.

Most of my long-time friends got married and raised their kids during my years of travelling the world and now, decades later when we speak on the phone or meet up, it feels like it was last week that we last spoke or got together. Not only is it the best feeling to reunite with a true friend we have not seen for a while but it is amazing how easy it is to pick up where we left off no matter how many years have passed.

Celebrate ...

~ele~

On land most people have weekly routines; they have a scheduled workweek and scheduled time off. On ships, we work seven days a week, three to seven months straight, during sea days and port days, and quite often not knowing what day of the week it is! Holidays are just another workday with added festivities to organize, execute and attend, all without missing a beat – that is our routine. Ship life has no Mondays thru Fridays, no weekends, no holidays, and no days off. Nevertheless what sets us apart is that we do get to celebrate, all the time, if not attending a ship event, the crew is always looking for a reason to celebrate.

Just a few of our 1,001 reasons to celebrate while working onboard a cruise ship…

~ *Someone is arriving – welcome or reunion of long lost friends*
~ *Somebody's birthday*
~ *National holiday celebration – there is one for each country*
~ *Religious holidays – we celebrate them all together and in peace*
~ *Name days – the Greeks have the best name-day parties*
~ *Someone has been promoted*
~ *Caribbean, Latin, Reggie, Balkan night etc. in the Crew Bar*
~ *The end of an extremely busy day*
~ *Great sales/great ratings*

~ *A port day tomorrow*
~ *Surviving a long or challenging day (lots of those)*
~ *A special meal with friends*
~ *An evening to chill with friends*
~ *Spa night, movie night, karaoke night, wine and cheese night*
~ *Somebody feels like it – that happens almost daily*
~ *Someone is leaving – the last night of the cruise is always a celebration for many*

The nice thing about celebrating onboard and with the crew was that the only planning necessary was what to wear, which bar to meet at, what time and maybe a cake. The ease of celebrating was one of the reasons that we did it so frequently. How frequently? Well, it could be as often as daily for many. Since we lived in such close quarters and a party was always in the making, trying to have a getaway from it all could be a challenge. One night Tom called to see what I was doing, I chuckled and said, "I'm going to stay in my room for the night and not drink just to prove that I can do it." I did succeed on that occasion and enjoyed watching a couple of movies while relaxing in bed.

The following night, I was celebrating once again; I hosted the Connoisseur Table and yes, this was a part of the job. This is where the guests pay to experience extraordinary cuisine with wine pairing for each course at the Captain's Table. I have also hosted the Chef's Table, a similar event; I would dine with guests in the galley while it was in full operation, which also included wine pairing, exclusive desserts and a special visit from the Executive Chef as well as other Senior Officers. Other work-related venues included cocktail parties, dining with guests as well as joining guests when invited for coffee or for drinks. Socializing is not just a part of our life onboard; it is our life onboard.

Music ...

∿

**There's no limit to where it can go
and where it can reach! – Alicia Keys**

We had just finished dinner and Mom was checking to see what was on TV. Coming from the living room I heard her yell out with excitement, "Paul Anka is on!" He is a Canadian teen idol of the 60s and a distinguished inductee into the Canadian Music Hall of Fame. Despite having such hits as *"Diana," "Lonely Boy," "Put Your Head on My Shoulder,"* and *"(You're) Having My Baby,"* it was his rendition of *"My Way"* that made the hairs on my arms and neck stand up! The words *"Regrets, I've had a few, but then again, too few to mention, I did what I had to do …and did it my way!"* best describe me and hearing it once again I had to remark, "When I depart this world, please play this song at my service."

Music has a way of evoking our memories, awakening our senses and giving definition to our feelings. Some songs such as *"Some of God's Greatest Gifts," "The River"* and *"The Dance"* by Garth Brooks contain lyrics reflecting life and a blueprint for living life. Then there are lyrics of an entire song that seem as if they were written for you and you alone. Giannis and I shared a few songs that marked various passages in our relationship; songs that defined our feelings at that moment in time. Even to this day when I hear certain songs, *"There You'll Be"* by Faith Hill and *"I*

Will always Love You" by Whitney Houston or Dolly Parton, I am immediately transported back in time as I relive some beautiful as well as some distant painful memories.

Many of us, at times, can find life challenging; we are trying to define who we are and what our place in the world is. Sometimes on our journey, we hear a song, not just any song, but the song that defines us; the song that puts things into perspective for us and helps pull us through, even if solely to release our bottled up emotions.

Working in a world of such diversity gave us the opportunity to become familiar with and truly appreciate various types of music from around the world, even if we could not understand the lyrics. With many of the Senior Officers being Greek there was energetic and melodious Greek music during celebrations, echoing from the offices as well as emanating from our cabins. It was not only the infectious tunes but also the love and the pride that the Greeks have for their country that made me such a fan of their music, and I still am to this day. The crew bar and the Independence Day celebrations held throughout the year for the various nationalities would also greatly expand our appreciation for music from around the globe. It was not unusual for the whole room in the crew bar to immediately jump out of our chairs to dance to the current Caribbean, European or Asian chart-toppers – just to name a few. Still to this day, thanks to friends and colleagues throughout my career I have a great love for various genres of music!

Music touches our very soul, has a way of reaching our depths and moves us in a way that nothing else can.

Illness ...

March 2010... As I sat sipping my coffee in the Charleston airport, I took some time to reflect on a very stressful contract, which I had just completed. Since November we had been sailing to the Caribbean and the Bahamas out of Baltimore. After a few months of encountering some cold weather ports in the north-eastern US, we were now changing the itinerary and would be departing out of Charleston, heading south via warmer ports of call. The winter season and winter travellers can bring viruses and being on a ship does not make you immune; in fact, it does the opposite. We are in an enclosed space with recycled air and with the possibility of travellers unknowingly arriving infected, this is just another type of storm that can happen on the high seas. Norovirus is something that is not taken lightly on ships. If someone arrives on board with this illness and if it is not dealt with swiftly it spreads like wildfire, and this March it did and with some far reaching consequences.

It takes some painstaking efforts on behalf of everyone onboard, guests included, to battle a virus like this. A Red Code takes effect when a certain percentage of people onboard become infected. When this occurs, everyone, guests and crew, is required to assist in the well-being of their fellow shipmates.

This particular winter season was especially bad; we encountered several Red Codes during these cruises. We performed sanitation barriers every embarkation day, which meant sanitizing the vessel from bow to stern, top to bottom and everywhere in between. We did everything in our power in an attempt to stop the virus from spreading. We even went to the extent of removing salt and pepper shakers from the tables and having to serve the buffet food to the guests and crew, all in an attempt to limit the spread of the virus. Our situation was dire; the CDC (Center for Disease Control) was involved, as was a special task force that was brought in from our head office. One of our cruises had to be cut short and the following cruise was delayed for two days in an attempt to get control of the invisible virus once and for all.

I was scheduled to go on vacation at the end of the last cruise, but the severity of the situation did not allow for new crew to embark so I was asked if I was willing to extend for an additional cruise. I didn't know until the last minute if I would be able to disembark, fortunately for me, I was. I knew that no matter what my vacation was about to hold, it was going to be a good one and that I was going to thoroughly enjoy the peace and the quiet! As far as that particular outbreak situation, it was conquered and life at sea got back to normal.

Live ...

~elle~

April 2010... I entered the living room wearing a blue, green and red flannel pyjama top; badly matched with blue and white PJ bottoms and to crown things off, my hair was covered in red hair dye! As I took stock of my appearance and by the look on Mom's and Janice's faces, I said, "I couldn't do this if I had a man in my life." The room erupted in laughter, and then I thought about what I said and decided to rephrase it to, "Yes I could if he had a great sense of humour." Well here I was, this was a snippet of my life and I have no regrets. Later that day I had a phone chat with my friend Clare, I regaled her with my adventures and experiences since I last saw her in October. Once again I was in awe as I reviewed the past six months of my life.

I began thinking back to New Year's Eve and how I spent time contemplating my life; what does the foreseeable future hold for me? So many wonderful things had transpired; I renewed a lucrative contract, the company was doing well and trips were being booked, I was assigned an assistant to help with the increased workload, time flew by and life was good. I began experiencing some unrest and trepidation; however, I do remember saying to myself, "What's meant to be will be." That realization put me in a state of peace with my life and my decisions.

Ahead of us we only have the unknown,
which is a field of infinite possibilities.

New Year's Eve saw me making a commitment to quit smoking, once again. A member of the casino staff overheard my plans and offered me a self-help book, *Allen Carr's, The Easy Way to Quit Smoking*. The book challenges all that we have learned. It teaches us that we do not have to be ruled by our minds, that we can step back from our thoughts and make conscious choices about what we do in our lives. It confirms that anything we are taught to believe can be untaught. I began reading it that evening and to my surprise, the book recommended not quitting smoking until the final chapter. The following morning I went to the smoking-room, book in hand, I sat down with my cup of coffee and lit up a cigarette. The room burst into hysterical laughter and I was taken aback. It took me a moment to catch on to what was happening and before I could exhale the smoke from my lungs someone said, "I thought you were quitting today!" At that moment as the wave of laughter continued and the question was posed, I began feeling extremely let down by the reaction of my friends and fellow crewmates. I explained how this book has a process to quitting smoking and everyone laughed once again. I was steadfast and read the book in six days, had my last cigarette on January 6th, and this time I knew in my heart that it was the final attempt in this lifetime.

To this day I am not sure if it was the book, the response from my shipmates, my health or if I was just tired of failing. Whatever it was, more than 10 years have now passed since that incredibly successful day and I have had no desire whatsoever to pick up the habit again. If anyone is still smoking and wants to quit, I highly recommend this book – guaranteed it will be the best $15 you will ever spend!

Decisions ...

ele

By June of 2010, the cruise industry was struggling with the sudden economic downturn. A few months prior I felt as if I were on the moon; sales were great, the cruises were booked, and I had an assistant. I began having an internal conversation with myself, which led me on a path to some deep and serious reflection.

After a long walk where I explored new sections of Piraeus, a suburb of Athens, Greece, I stopped for lunch at a little Greek taverna. The *taverna* was on the edge of a small park the size of a city block, which overlooked grass, a footpath, a stone wall and a small pond. As I sat eating my octopus salad, red pepper and olive spread with fresh bread and a fresh Greek salad, while sipping a glass of local white, I began to think; "Am I fighting off depression?" I was living my dream, yet I felt as if I were depressed.

Because of the economic downturn, people were tightening their purse strings and the pressure was on to increase sales. It is interesting how we can deal so well with some pressures in our lives, while others present a challenge. At this particular moment in time, the sales pressures for me were challenging. I needed to ask myself, "*Is where I am in my life still right for me?*" I still needed to work for a living and I realized that despite my challenges, I was still being paid to travel around the world. I knew deep down in my heart I was not ready to give that up. I could not foresee any possible career changes at this time; there was no other job that I wanted to have. I decided, be it right or wrong, for now, to appreciate the good things in my world, work through the challenging aspects and continue on. My internal conversation, however, did put me on the path to some serious thinking.

Wishes ...

~~ℓℓ~~

September 2010... Another contract was just about to end and I was spending my last days continuing to explore our homeport city of Piraeus. It was a glorious, warm, and sunny day with blue skies and that only added to my unequivocal love of Greece. I had stopped in at my favourite *taverna* for my last Greek lunch of the season; I was reliving this morning's events while listening to the local music. I was tasked by my shipmate Amy to compile a wish list and I was having a mental block as to what my number one wish would be. As I sat there contemplating what my wishes were my thoughts drifted to my encounter with Giannis and his family, earlier in the day.

While on my way to work I exited my corridor through the door which was in eyesight of the gangway; this is where the guests and crew enter and exit the ship. The very moment I exited I looked over and saw Giannis and his family boarding. He was travelling with his wife, their baby girl and his aunt. Upon the sight of him my stomach rose up into my throat, my mouth went dry and I am sure I was a bit lightheaded. I decided at that very second, to keep walking quickly; this was not the appropriate moment for greeting Giannis and his family. To my surprise, an hour later they passed by my office. I have to say that, in the end, I was very excited to not only see Giannis and his bride but also his aunt who I adored. We had met before and always had a wonderful time when I visited his family in Greece; she too was thrilled to see me again. However, I was most excited about finally getting to meet the baby, as I had seen many photos sent to me by the oh so proud dad! I honestly knew after that meeting, despite the break-up being very hard, that we had both done the right thing – what was right for each of us!

My wish list arose from having spent time training Amy in a newly-created position. During our training and chat sessions, she mentioned that she is a Reiki Master and told me that if I would make up my wish list that she would perform her Reiki on it. As odd as this may have sounded to me, for some strange reason, it was exactly what I wanted to hear so that evening I sat down to make my list. I had no idea at that time what my wish list would include because I had never been asked for or given any serious thought to a wish list. However, it was seeing Giannis and his daughter that allowed me to remember what my one and only first wish should be.

Number one on my wish list was meeting my soul mate. Until this point in life, I truly had not been ready to meet him. Had I met "Mr. Right" prior to this time, he would not have in the end been right for me; I believe that a relationship would not have endured. Not for anything that he or I would have said or done but because of the extensive changes and growth that I experienced through the years.

The second was to finish my book and to have it published. I realized after putting this wish in writing that I had fears of this wish coming true. My reason for wanting this second wish is based on the third wish on my list.

My third is big, and it is the reason for my second wish. My wish is to make a difference by helping to change this world for the better. How on earth am I going to make any of this happen? This is totally out of my comprehension at this time and yet my inner voice keeps telling me that it is what I want to achieve. I truly believe that somehow I am going to do something to make this wish a reality.

My last wish, which was an afterthought, was to remain youthful and to stay healthy. I realized as I was writing it down, that it is, in fact, the most important wish because if I do not have my health then I cannot possibly achieve any of the other goals.

Angels ...

ele

October 2010... I had disembarked the ship in Barcelona and was taken to the hotel, where I promptly checked in and dropped my luggage off in the room. My flight did not depart until 6 am the following morning, so I was headed into town to enjoy the afternoon and evening. As I exited the hotel en route to the bus station, I failed to see the decorative curb that was just on the outside of the lobby. Crash, Bam, Boom; down I fell. First, my left ankle twisted which dropped me onto both my knees and then thrust me forward to land on both of my wrists, then to collapse onto my left shoulder scraping it and then landing not so gracefully in the middle of the street. What I remember clearly, was that the entire encounter was totally silent and in slow motion. My glasses went flying and after feeling the final thud of my left cheekbone hitting the pavement, I just laid there with the wind knocked out of me. I could not move, paralyzed with fear of what damages had occurred. All I could do was watch helplessly as the hotel staff, taxi drivers, my crewmate and everyone else nearby rushed to my aid. They helped me up and took me into the hotel bar where they sat me down, gave me an ice pack and a glass of water. I sat for about a half-hour; nobody allowed me to move, and I was too afraid to venture anywhere. I sensed an angel was with me at that moment; how did I sustain such a nasty fall and walked away just about unscarred. My cheekbone swelled up to what felt like the size of a football, I could see it out of the corner of my eye, okay, it was more like the size of a lime, but it was still massive!

After regaining my wits, I realized that my glasses were broken and I went back to my room to find my backup set. I was determined that I was not going to let this incident dampen my precious time in Barcelona so I decided to go into town with some of the ship guests. I got on the shuttle bus; the bag of ice on my cheek and off we went. I left the guests downtown and despite the fact I had this massive lump on my face, I walked for hours and eventually sat on a patio, on the tree-lined busy pedestrian mall of *La Rambla* in Barcelona's city center and enjoyed a chilled glass of Sangria and some tapas. Despite my injuries, I was not going to miss experiencing all the glorious sights and sounds of spectacular Spain on a Saturday evening.

Another angel was with me the following morning. The alarm went off at 3:15 am; I got out of bed and made my way to the bathroom. I turned on the light and immediately looked in the mirror to survey the damage. Yikes, the left side of my face was black and blue and my cheekbone really did look like a football by morning. Despite my appearance, I had a 7:15 am flight to catch; I showered, packed up and caught the airport shuttle. While checking in, I was told that there was an additional fee for my extra bag; in my mind, that was not a problem. However payment had to be made by credit card or in Euros, I had neither; what I did have was US dollars. I was told that I could exchange the US for Euros at the exchange booth, ok, except the booth opened at 7 am, which meant that I would miss my flight. I was taken aback with this turn of events.

My last 24 hours had been challenging; first my fall, then my swollen face and now this! I imagined under all that black and blue, someone saw the worry on my face, or I was experiencing a great deal of sympathy because of my looks. Either way, I paused, trying to figure out what on earth to do next when a man gently said over my shoulder, "I'll take care of it." I turned around in total disbelief, I knew I could not decline the offer so despite being totally embarrassed, I said, "Thank you, please let me give you US funds." He smiled and politely said "It is not necessary." I did insist and as I handed him the money, which he did accept, then he surprised me and gave me half of it back!

Angels come in all forms; the strangers on the street who rush to your aid or the kind gentleman who opens his wallet to you. I truly believe our desire to help one another transcends race and culture.

Ethics ...

꙳

December 2012... Mom was vacationing in Mexico as she did every year beginning in November and I planned to spend a quiet Christmas and New Year's at home. I would be on land until the end of February and thought this would be a good opportunity to spend some time taking it easy, reading, writing, sleeping and watching TV. It sounded great until I realized that I would have to shop, cook, clean, do laundry and freeze my butt off in the middle of winter! I paused and asked myself, "What else can I do?" I decided moments later to go on a cruise.

I arrived home on December 17ᵗʰ and on the 21ˢᵗ I was on a flight to board a cruise of Southeast Asia. I chose three back-to-back cruises, which totalled just over one month. The first cruise took me to Indonesia; the highlight was the visit to Komodo Island where I was amazed by the sight of the infamous Komodo dragons. We also had an overnight stay in Bali giving us two full days to explore the island. The second cruise was to Thailand and Vietnam with two overnights in Bangkok, one overnight in each Ho Chi Minh City (formerly Saigon) and in Hanoi (Halong Bay). My third cruise was a reverse itinerary of the second cruise, however, I chose not to continue and the following is the bases for curtailing my vacation.

On the third day of the second cruise, while arriving in Bangkok, I received a call from a colleague and friend who was working onboard. She called to tell me there had been an issue with the complimentary Wi-Fi minutes that she had given me; she said that she had been reprimanded for doing so. Courtesies such as this had always been done in the business and we assumed that with my managerial position this would not be an issue, but it was. We both admitted to feeling terrible and extremely embarrassed for our indiscretion. The following morning as we were leaving the ship to explore the city, she was informed that she had a meeting scheduled for 6 pm that evening with the Captain. She was told at that time that it was not a Masters Hearing. A Masters Hearing happens just before a crewmember is dismissed. This type of meeting struck us both as extremely odd and neither of us believed for a second that this minor breach was going to end badly. The prevalent thought was that there would be only a verbal reprimand, so we felt free to laugh and joke about it while enjoying our lunch, joking that it may be our last, not honestly believing that it would be.

We returned for her 6 pm meeting and I asked her to call me when it was finished; by 7 pm I had not heard from her, so I decided to call her. She answered, politely and in a sombre voice said, "May I call you back?" At that moment my stomach did a complete summersault, I knew it was real – she was being dismissed. This was my long-time colleague and friend and I felt responsible.

When she finally called, it was confirmed, she had been let go and would be leaving the ship the following morning. Since I was a guest I was not able to say goodbye to her in person; I was left with watching her disembark the vessel from my cabin window. This was a very surreal and heartbreaking moment for me; her career was over while my vacation of a lifetime continued and I was devastated. I have never experienced such a deep and profound sadness for someone. I could not stop thinking of her as she packed her belongings, said goodbye to her boyfriend, her friends, leaving the ship, the wait at the airport and then arriving home to break the news to her family. It was unbearable knowing that I played a role in this unfathomable "mess." I was in tears for an entire week and it was agonizing to face anyone; I was unsure if I could complete this cruise or for that matter, the third cruise. Thanks to the kindness of my few friends onboard I was able to make it through my final days of this trip.

Shortly after her departure, despite being shaken by everything that had happened, I needed to do something so I decided that I would go into town and walk. My plan was to walk to the Banyan Tree hotel to watch the sunset and panoramic view from the 61st floor, this would give me a lot of time and space to walk and think. I decided that I would take a couple of hours to tour the city sights via the Chao Phraya River before doing so. I boarded one of the local boats and my plan was to head in one direction for about an hour and then return. I had no clue where I was going; however, as the crowds began thinning out, I decided that I would go one more stop. Fifteen minutes later I was at the end of the route, I got off the boat, looked around and realized that I could not find a boat that was returning. At one point as I attempted to board the next boat when it arrived, I was told via hand gestures that there is no boarding. The boat which arrived after that also went out of service. I took stock of my situation; I had travelled far away from the city to the suburbs where no one spoke English, I was unfamiliar with the surroundings and I had travelled in the opposite direction of where the ship was docked. I felt some trepidation; it was late in the day and the "What ifs" took over. What if there is no boat returning to the city, and what if I found a taxi but the driver did not speak English and what if I could not approximate where the ship was docked, and if I was lucky it would only cost me $200 – *if* I was lucky! I reminded myself that we were here overnight so I had until tomorrow evening to get back. That is what was great about this!

I kept attempting to speak to people. I could feel that I was starting to appear somewhat panicked, and I was aware that people around were watching me. Eventually, a young man looked at me, I had no idea what he said, but he smiled and directed me to the far corner of the pier. Within 10 minutes a boat was there and I was on my way back towards downtown. As I settled into my seat I began to feel my heart beating at a somewhat normal pace again, it was then I realized that I was seated for the start of a spectacular sunset. Although not the 61st floor of the Banyan Tree hotel, it was, nevertheless, a sight I will never forget. I watched the various pastel colours of the sunset descending behind the palaces and temples and each turn brought a new jaw-dropping view. It was an extraordinary trip back down the river and by the time I returned to where I originally started it was dark which allowed for an incredible view of this remarkable city at night. I chose to end my adventure by sitting on a patio with a glass of wine and took the time to replay the events of the past 48 hours.

The following day I was scheduled to escort a tour, and despite not wanting too, I could not back out now. The thought of enjoying myself under these circumstances was not possible, even though I was in Bangkok for the first and maybe last time in my life. As I reviewed the Wi-Fi issues I had to take ownership for my part; I had wanted to post about my vacation on Facebook and someone lost her job for it. I did my best not to focus on all the complementary services and extra free courtesies that we give to our guests and sometimes to other staff; why are these not called out. Why was this issue resolved in this manner? This did not mean that I wanted others punished; it just meant that I did not feel she deserved the sentence she received. We both believed that the charge would be overturned once we explained ourselves and she would return to another ship in the future.

I was not happy and not feeling comfortable in my surroundings despite the fact that very few people knew what had actually happened. However, I decided to cut my vacation short by one cruise. I rode out my time onboard and spent a few days in Hong Kong before returning home.

I believe that this incident was possibly the most unjust event that I have had to experience personally. She was not rehired, despite various attempts made by both of us and was unemployed for an entire year. She eventually found work outside of the cruise industry. I have finally healed and although we have not discussed the incident again, I truly hope she has healed as well.

Realization ...

From my perspective the next two years seemed unproductive, nothing new and exciting was happening in my life. I was still in the same career, my colleagues kept getting younger, I seemed to fall into one disappointing relationship after another and I did not feel that I was moving ahead with any aspect of my life. I would question myself; "Was I experiencing a midlife crisis, was I losing it, or, was it possible that I was just ready to move on and take my life to the next level?" Whatever the reason that stoked these feelings, I realized that I was no longer feeling that I was really where I was meant to be. I could feel that I was not being true to myself.

In retrospect, I now know that I had come to another fork in the road. This was a wakeup call for me to take stock of my life. The questions arising were, "Was I where I wanted to be at this time in my life, does my lifestyle meet my needs and is all that I am doing in my day-to-day life for the right reasons? Was I still moving in the right direction and doing what was right for me?" Interestingly, the answers which at one time were yes to all of the above, had now, for various reasons, changed to no!

> *Sometimes all we know is what we do not want*
> *and that is often enough to go on.*

I had always thought that working in the cruise industry would take me to the next level in my life, but now, I was not so sure. I knew that I wanted to complete my book; although at this time I had no idea how it was going to end or where it would take me next. My inner voice was still telling me to continue my writing mission. I was not, however, for whatever reason, able to find the motivation to do it while onboard.

I realized that a few more years would mark my 20-year anniversary working onboard and travelling the world. I would receive a substantial payout from the company and that staying until then would give me a little more time to visit places which I had not yet seen while getting paid. Therefore … I continued working.

Passion ...

∼ello∼

If you do what you love and love what you do, your passion will be reflected in your actions. That passion is evident in the people throughout the cruise industry and in all the various positions onboard.

What caught my attention on this particular day was my interaction with Issy. Issy is one of the most delightful people I have had the privilege of knowing and working with. She was an assistant cleaner onboard and if you had the pleasure of crossing paths with her you were fortunate. Issy is a tall slender woman, who walks with her head held high and always wears a great big sincere smile on her face. Her infectious upbeat greeting brings sunshine to a cloudy day; she truly brightened mine on each and every encounter.

One particular evening, as I was leaving the main guest dining room, I heard my name. I turned around and there was this beautiful Honduran woman doing her *little "I love life" attitude dance*, and that was Issy! As I walked towards the restroom, where she stood, I felt two arms embrace my waist; Issy looked down at me and said, "I love you, Laura." As strange as this encounter may sound, for her and me this was anything but strange. She is one of the most beautiful souls I have ever met. She is not only pleasant, but she is also outgoing, energetic, loving, caring, funny and so much more. Issy has been known for opening the door to the restroom, affectionately greeting guests with her contagious smile while proudly saying, "Welcome to my office!"

Issy is one of the most inspirational and fun-loving authentic souls with an unsurpassable passion for life. Anyone who entered Issy's life was moved by her warmth and love!

Success ...

How do we define success? According to the dictionary, one definition is; the accomplishment of an aim or purpose. Success, however you define it, is a wonderful place to be, especially if you have put your heart and soul into attaining it and if you sought it out for the right reasons. The definition of success is different for each of us, and it changes as we evolve.

Do you work to live or live to work? The old saying, *"Do what you love and the money will follow"* has always worked on my behalf and interestingly in both of my careers, since I have worked for the love of the work. Making money, despite being a necessity, was secondary to the passion I had for the cruise industry. My definition of success at that time was living your dream and getting paid to do it and I have always slept very well knowing that what I did for a living, I did for the right reasons. However, I realized that I had now played this game for as long as I wanted to. I have seen how the pressure to look successful has driven people to extravagance; they seem to chase money and fame for all the wrong reasons. This has caused me to pause and take stock, not only of the world around me but of my life as well.

I have had two careers, both in sales; it was fun, the people were great and there was a desire to succeed *in* my job, but now there is the pressure to succeed *at* my job. It was my job to fill those cabins on the ships and the pressure grew with each passing year. I began to realize that I was now living to work and not working to live. I absolutely loved my career and I am extremely grateful for all that it provided career-wise and for me personally, nevertheless, I knew that it was time for me to move on. I believe that it is very important to do what we love and if our hearts are in it, we can give 100 percent. If however, we are in a place in our lives where our hearts are elsewhere, it can be a recipe for disaster; we grow disinterested, develop stress, exhaustion, burnout, depression or more, none of which provide a healthy balanced life.

In the midst of all these changes; younger crew, the pressure to sell, ageing and loss of passion, I knew that not only was the world around me changing but that the world within me was changing as well. I wanted something new, something different, and something beyond all that I currently had. Looking back I realize that I was not giving up on what was, but rather realizing that it was once again time to take my life to a new level so that I could continue to grow.

Demons ...

〜ello〜

WHETHER IT IS...

Chocolate/ice cream/pizza
Shopping/gambling/hoarding
Cigarettes/alcohol/prescription pills
Marijuana/cocaine/heroine
Sex/porn/adultery
Negativity/gossip/judging/dishonesty
Fear/pain/stress/guilt/insecurity
Laziness/procrastination/complacency
Greed/control/money/stuff

Today when I reflect back on my life in general and my life at sea, I have fond and cherished memories. I have been blessed with a life of joy, adventure, excitement and an incredible education – thus the subtitle *The World as my Classroom*. However my joyful, adventurous life and education did not preclude me from being aware and experiencing some of the darkness which life sheds on us and this is why I chose to write about demons.

Why is it that at times, our lives become so challenging, or as we like to refer to it as "messed up," and cause us such grief and suffering? We all have free will, the opportunity to do as we please; everything we do in life, every step we take along the way, we have a choice. We all know deep down, through our little voice from within, what we should and should not do. I do not believe that there are too many of us out there running around without a conscience. If we indulge in one of the many joys in life, eating, drinking, sex and shopping just to name a few, without feeling a sense of guilt then we know that what we are doing is for the right reason – to enjoy life.

When we hear our little voice telling us that we should not indulge because we will suffer the consequences later, we know that what we are doing is strictly for instant gratification. At that moment we are ignoring a warning which may ultimately lead to the consequences of our decisions. Again at any given moment we have choices; we can – right now – endure the discomfort of discipline or we can – later – endure the pain and guilt of regret.

Today, I realize that I have yet to meet anyone that has not been or is not currently consumed with some of these "demons" and that I, despite seeing it all so clearly, still battle with making correct choices. A friend recently said, "You are so hard on yourself," a statement which my mom confirmed. After a lot of thought about why I would project this image, I realized that I am hard on myself. Why, because I really want to evolve, live the next chapter of my life being my true and authentic self. I am aware that on occasion I choose in favour of instant gratification; indulging in a long-time habit or because I am just simply taking the easy route over a more challenging one. However, I do pride myself for all of the occasions in which I have made good and healthy choices in my life.

I have to chuckle at how most of us go through life believing that the day is going to come when we are going to feel like doing the right thing. It is unfortunate that many of us wait for something to go drastically wrong before we make the right choice, knowing deep down that the right decision will ultimately lead to positive and advantageous changes in our lives.

Love ...

~ele~

I give credit to my worldly education for teaching me self-love. Because I learned to love myself does not mean that it is a closed chapter. On the contrary, I have found that to live consciously and apply what we have learned is an entirely new ball game. We have internal conversations and those conversations can be damaging to our well-being. For example, we may ask ourselves, "Why am I so fat?" If you ask a question in that manner, of course, the answer is going to be negative because there is no positive answer to that question. Think about it. The only positive answer is "You are not fat" and if you truly believed that, you would not be having the conversation with yourself in the first place! We need to start asking better questions such as; *"What does my body need to look or feel better or how can I treat myself better today than I did yesterday?"* It may not work on the first attempt. Your answer may be "Who cares" or "I'll have pizza!" Even the second or third attempt might be a response you do not like, however, eventually your answers will change and they *will* become positive.

> ***Whether we think we can or we cannot – we are right! –***
> ***Henry Ford***

We are *all* special, uniquely different and precious. It is actually amusing how we can see the good qualities in others but, unfortunately, too often we cannot see them in ourselves and I believe this is where our problems start. If we do not appreciate ourselves, love ourselves and we do not take care of ourselves, this is the beginning of our self-sabotaging. It is very important that we pay attention to our thoughts and internal dialogue. It is pertinent to remember we are merely the observers of our thoughts – we are not our thoughts.

In order for us to move forward, we must accept ourselves today, as we are, and then with a positive attitude move toward achieving anything that we set our minds to. We must remember that to achieve success we must wake up feeling good, loving ourselves *now* which will start our day on the right foot. These are a few cherished quotes I have accumulated over the years from various wise souls. Not sure who to attribute them to, but they are good reminders worth keeping at the forefront of our minds:

Yesterday is done and gone, cannot be brought back
or changed.
Fear is just a projection of the future – a vision in
our minds.
Courage is feeling fear and doing it anyway.
Today is a brand new act and we are the directors!

My favourite reminder to start my day:

A fulfilled life begins with self-love. In loving and accepting
all of yourself, you can then be able to openly love and
accept others in all their beauty and glory. – Louise Hay

Behaviours ...

ele

Throughout my life, whether it was on ships or on land, I have engaged in poor behaviours. I spoke and thought negatively while looking for the bad or the downside of things. I was controlling and my personal favourite was expecting everyone not only to see things my way but also to act accordingly. These are all behaviours, which were learned at some point or another in my life. The good news is that if we learn a behaviour then we can *unlearn* it as well. I, again, thank Allen Carr for teaching me the first lessons on how to unlearn a behaviour.

A lot of our habits are rooted in our behaviours. The first step is to acknowledge the negative patterns of behaviour in your life. Dr. Phil always says, *"You can't fix something that you don't acknowledge!"* This is a perfect exercise in taking a good look at ourselves instead of focusing on others.

The second step is to explore why; why do we have the particular behaviour and that is the tough step. When you are being totally honest with yourself, you need to remember one thing – *nobody is listening – except for you and God and you do not have to impress either.* Therefore, you have absolutely no reason to lie!

Once you acknowledge that the behaviour exists; now ask yourself, "What *can I do to change this habit?"* If any negativity gets into the conversation acknowledge it and try again until a positive response arises and then write it down. Regardless of how long it takes – do not give up!

If we are not getting good answers
we need to ask ourselves better questions.

Being able to claim responsibility for my actions has allowed me the ease and comfort to ask myself those probing questions. I regularly ask myself what I can do to change a certain behaviour or habit.

For most of my life, I was a master of *to-do lists.* I was convinced that because of them I was totally in control, that someday I was going to master everything pending in my life.

I have always wanted to keep a journal and have not to this day completed that task; this is something I regret. One of my journal attempts started January 1st, 2014, which came complete with, of course, my New Year's to-do list.

The first month passed then the second, and then into the third. The journaling fizzled out. I did, on occasion, do some of the tasks, but all in all, I finally came to the brilliant conclusion that I did not do well journaling but I also did not do well with to-do lists. I realized that I found them overwhelming; accordingly, this was the reason for my mastery of procrastination. I felt guilty; how can I change this behaviour. It was suggested to me that instead of having a list, I should schedule a project. I incorporated this new approach and not only does it work but also it makes for a much more pleasant, more productive guilt-free day.

Have I overcome procrastination? It is still a work in progress, along with other behaviours, beliefs and habits. I think that in overcoming many of my personal challenges and in losing a few makes for a much brighter life. The alternative is attempting none and suffering from complacency, guilt and a lack of fulfillment.

A to-do list is a list of all the things you didn't do yesterday, probably won't get around to doing today, and will feel bad about not having done tomorrow!

I also ask myself; *"What can I focus on that is positive, and what will make me feel good?"*

Here is my list of positives that help me feel good about life and reinforce positive behaviours.

Nature/beaches/wildlife
Love/Peace/serenity
Energize/take action/educate
Give something to someone/give something away
Relax, breathe, enjoy precious moments and just watch the world go by
Positive attitude/appreciation/uplifting others
Be nice to someone
Drink plenty of water or healthy beverage options
Exercise/walk/read/meditate/garden
Prepare and eat healthy foods options

Feeling bad? Then pick something good to focus on.

Stillness ...

ele

I have a mind that does not quit; it is always thinking multiple thoughts all at once. I would be having one conversation with the person in front of me and another conversation within me simultaneously; yikes, it can be busy in my head. Thanks to, once again, Eckhart Tolle and his book *The Power of Now*, I have learned to quiet the internal chatter. At times, when I concentrate, I can stop the chatter and bring a certain quiet to my mind.

To reach that place of quiet and calm in your mind, you need to start with a quiet spot without interruptions, get comfortable and open your mind to your thoughts and then listen. Allow your thoughts to speak, to reveal their nature to you, pay close attention and listen to exactly what your thoughts are saying. If we start paying attention to our thoughts, practicing and focusing every night before going to sleep and then when we wake up, we will begin to see that we are not our thoughts – rather, we are observing our thoughts!

You are now in the position of the observer and can take control of your thoughts. My method of coping came about from a desire to learn and understand myself, my interest in other people's experiences and trial and error to discern what works for me. *Press Pause* – when the thoughts were relentless, I would say to myself "Press pause." This would immediately stop the thought process and I would begin to acknowledge the stillness. In the beginning, the quiet was only for a second or two, and then the thoughts would edge their way back in. Nevertheless, with practice the duration of the silence became longer. As with most arts, you need practice. Today after years of focusing on my inner peace, I can say that I am able to tune out the unwanted thoughts and replace them with pleasant thoughts and imagery or choose to think about nothing! Meditation anyone?

Sensational ...

⌇

Eighteen years into my amazing career I finally had the opportunity to work onboard during an Atlantis Charter. What made this opportunity so exciting were the guests; I felt and understood their exuberance for life. For the past 18 years, it was my pleasure to greet and assist individuals, couples and families from all corners of the earth. Atlantis is a company that specializes in gay charters and only a few are hosted each year. For those who are unaware of exactly what this means, it is that our entire guest list, with the exception of a handful of women, was men – 2,000 men! This was an opportunity to immerse myself in a culture that I had only seen from the fringes. As with every cruise there are diverse personalities; some people wear their essence in their clothing, mannerisms or speech and others, you may not even notice. Men in all shapes, sizes, colours, ethnicities, ages and different walks of life were onboard. As diverse as the group was, they shared two very special commonalities; a sense of pride and electrifying positive energy. The sheer excitement of our guests was from knowing that in addition to a dream cruise, each and every guest was free to be who they truly were and have the experience of a lifetime.

Normally at the start of a cruise, very few people make eye contact or say hello, and this is to be expected until they understand ship culture. A guest will always be greeted with a salutation, followed by a "How is your day?" from every member of the crew.

After hearing this repeatedly, a guest finally succumbs to being acknowledged and now they are comfortable to make eye contact and conversation. This cruise was a complete 180 – not only did our guests say "Hello," but they made eye contact long enough for a positive conversation to be taken further, and that was an amazing feeling.

These particular cruises have gained a reputation for being "wild and anything goes!" It was not hard to see why; the Atlantis Cruise Director and the Captain set the tone at boat drill. As it was Norovirus season it was important to remind our guests of the precautions they should take. However, no opportunity was missed for innuendo! *"Wash your hands, wash your hands, wash your hands and wash anything before putting it in your mouth,"* was the announcement. Another statement was, *"Take it inside!"* Those *reminders* kept coming for the entire cruise. I was left with a chuckle after each announcement, it kept the energy level high and it was a reminder about health and safety in a humorous way.

The first theme party was "Glow." The energy was palpable and grew even more intense as you approached the pool deck where the party was taking place. Walking through the door of the upper deck you were met with an explosion of light and sound and energy to match. Imagine if you can, 2,000 men dancing around a pool, under the open night sky. Strobe lights were flashing, the smoke machine was smokin', the music was thumping and when you looked up as far as you could see, there were laser lights dancing with the stars. Truly, this was mind blowing to watch. "Treasure Island" night was just as impressive with incredible costumes, music, lights, and energy.

One afternoon as I was on my way to get a cup of tea I decided to see what was happening out on deck. This is where I came upon the most interesting party of them all, the afternoon "Rainbow Party." The outfits were in the rainbow theme, which allowed for everyone in various stages of dress and undress to proudly display their strategically placed body art. I have never seen so many beautiful and uninhibited men in one place; there was plenty of love to go around. This was not the first time on this cruise that I felt that I had died and gone to heaven, and ended up amidst the most gorgeous men ever!

Last night of the cruise: the final big party was approaching. There had been an event every night for the past six days and as exciting, crazy and over the top as it had been the atmosphere was ramping up for the final big extravaganza – White Night. This was a monochromatic party; from white angel wings, sequined jock-straps, to white shorts and sneakers and outlandish coordinated costume. This outdid any New Year's Eve I have experienced in my lifetime.

As impressive as the parties and costumes were, that was nothing compared to the glowing personalities of the guests. Many of them would just approach you and start chatting. They would ask, "*How does the crew feel about having our group onboard?*" We were constantly being told, "*We love you guys for having us,*" and our response, said with absolute genuineness was, "*We love you guys!*" Most conversations would end with hugs and sincere affection from attractive men … again - *life is good!*

Appreciation ...

‿ℓℓ‿

Sometimes you need the insight of others to see your own magnificence! The Captain was being transferred to another ship and he and his wife came by to say good-bye. We were chatting and she said to me "You are an inspiration!" I chuckled, as that is the last thing that I would have said about myself. I asked her why she would say that. She told me that I am always positive and that I have such an appreciation for life. I stopped and thought about it and came to the realization that this is something that people often say to me.

I acknowledge that I have a grand appreciation for so much of what this incredible life has to offer; interestingly it is the little things in life that we should truly appreciate and surprisingly they are free. So, I asked myself, "What exactly *do* I appreciate in life?" I made a list and I found that if I just read it slowly, taking the time to pause at each word, and bring the vision into my mind, it brings me peace. I invite you to make your own list and meditate on what you appreciate in life.

This is my list:

Sunrises and sunsets
Flowers, trees, plants and the smell of fresh-cut grass
The silence of snowfalls and the sound of rain
The sea, the sky, the clouds

Mountains, canyons, beaches, forests, waterfalls and rivers
The sight and sound of small children laughing
Watching people in love and people dancing
Listening to music
Being in love
Watching wildlife
Being greeted by your pet when arriving home
and feeling their unconditional love
Planes flying – ships floating
The smell of fresh baked goods or home-cooked food
Enjoying quality family time
Talking to a good friend
Enjoying special occasions
Watching a good movie, snuggled up with a loved one, your kids,
pets, a blanket or a favourite stuffed animal
Enjoying laughs and tasty beverages with friends
Seeing the smile on the face of a stranger
Clean laundry
Laughing
Savouring favourite foods with a glass of wine
Sitting in a foreign country or your own watching the world go by
Listening to a story of someone else's positive life experience
Watching kids grow up
Watching your friends grow old, while you do not age a bit until
you look at old photos
A nice hot bath or shower
Reading a good book
Ancient Ruins
Spectacular landmarks
The aroma and taste of a good cup of coffee
A look, a touch, a hug, a kiss
Everything else in this amazing world and all it has to offer!

We only live once, no one has a guarantee and the future is unknown to each and every one of us. As I was writing this chapter Malaysia Airlines Flight 370 had just disappeared into the ocean with 263 souls onboard. There was also the recent abduction of 200 Nigerian schoolgirls by Boko Haram. Shortly after those international horror stories, Malaysia Airlines Flight 17 from Amsterdam to Kuala Lumpur was shot down over eastern Ukraine. These were just a few of the atrocities that were happening around the world at that particular moment in time. Although we refuse to believe it when we are young, time really does fly, making life a lot shorter than we could possibly imagine even when all goes well and as we planned. I intend to keep my personal appreciation list close by and continue to add to it ensuring that I don't forget how precious a gift today truly is.

Tests ...

_ele,

LIFE IS A JOURNEY!

I choose to use the words grateful and appreciation regularly. I apply these two adjectives to describe all that I have been so fortunate to have and continue to receive and experience. I am thankful that I have the ability to learn from others and from my own lessons, many of which have taken the greater part of my life, and those, which I am still currently working through.

I believe that life is packed with hundreds of lessons because life is a journey with assignments along the way and not a destination. If we do not pass a test when it is presented to us, that test *will* appear again. Somewhere down the road, we will be given the opportunity once again to pass that test, and if we do not, this process will continue until we do get it.

My inner voice has been speaking to me throughout my life; the problem was that I spent most of the time either ignoring it or instead listening to my ego and allowing it to run the show. One of the best examples of my internal conversations would have to be my love life. When I look back on my relationships, I can recall my inner voice having an opinion about each of them and despite hearing some subtle warnings, I chose to act on my ego's opinion. Looking back I can see that my inner voice was right every time. I received such information as, *"A nice guy but not for you,"* *"Watch out this one's bad news,"* the most popular, *"He's way too young for you,"* or *"Why on earth would you even think to go there?"* This is another perfect example of going for instant gratification (looking for love in all the wrong places) and ignoring the obvious long-term harmful effects. I was with friends and they were talking about their honeymoons, where they had gone and what they had done; I piped up and said, "I've never had a honeymoon" to which my best friend responded, "You've had lots!" Her response was born from the fact that I have never been married and that I have had a life full of very interesting relationships. Do I have regrets for not listening to my inner voice? Not really – I have had an intriguing love life, dated some really great guys (you know who you are) and I've learned some extremely valuable lessons with the not so great ones. All in all – making me the caring independent woman that I am today!

What I do know is that by finally acknowledging my inner voice and realizing that it is always right, I have learned to listen to it. I can stop going to those places where I keep repeating the same unnecessary and sometimes painful lessons.

Action ...

~elle.

December 2014... Three days before the ship was scheduled to arrive in Cairns, Australia, I was sitting at my desk and a member of my team walked up and said, "Let's go skydiving!" I stopped, thought about it and heard my inner voice say, *"If you don't take this opportunity now, you'll never do it!"* I paused and then said, "If you guys want to, I'll go." Three days later, we were at the airfield, receiving our instructions while waiting for the first group to return from their jump. The first group expressed exhilaration and excitement, *"This was amazing,"* was the consensus. You would think that the responses upon their return would make one feel better about one's decision, but no, they did not. Nevertheless, we boarded the plane. Upon take-off, I was still okay. It was not until we were flying parallel with the clouds and still rising that I began to feel queasy. As we flew higher I began to realize that there was no way out and it would be embarrassing making a scene at this point. I decided to focus on the beautiful view of the Great Barrier Reef below and kept breathing deeply while acknowledging the very active butterflies in my stomach! A few minutes later, the hatch opened, I could feel my heart pounding in my chest and before I knew it the first team was out followed by the second and then it was my turn. Off we went; yes, I really did jump out of a plane at 14,000 feet. I think this is going to go down as the wildest thing I have ever done or will ever do in my entire life. It is exactly as you would envision it to be. You are assisted out of the plane; ok, truly you are heaved out by the person you're attached too. We were in a string of people; there were six of us, and six pros securely attached to us from behind – we hoped! It took approximately three minutes between the first jumpers and the last to jump from the plane.

The moment you exit the plane, you begin freefalling for a minute – the longest minute in my life! The feeling of exhilaration and fear rushed through my body as I descended through the clouds towards the earth with no parachute. I think if I had been alone, without a pro, my heart would have stopped two seconds after departing the plane. Then I realized that I was truly living in the moment, living in the now. During the decent, which was an extremely long moment of insanity, I just kept slowly repeating to myself "Breathe real deep and try to enjoy the experience."

> **Fear resides in anticipation and dissipates**
> **only when you can no longer resist what is.**

I learned that fear only resides in anticipation, because the moment you jump, although it is an adrenaline rush, the fear dissipates the second you realize that there is no turning back and that you can no longer resist what is. I am thrilled that I did it, and I now say, *"If I can jump out of a plane, I can do anything!"*

The skydiving event was another pivotal moment in my life. I realized not long afterward that if we are going to move forward with *anything* in life we **First... have to take action!** Does it mean that I don't experience fear anymore? Absolutely not, but when I do, I can remind myself of the definition of courage: *feeling fear and doing it anyway*. Remember that anticipation is the worst part of anything that we have to face. Once you take the necessary action the actual doing it is never as bad as we envisioned it to be. Such as jumping out of the plane, when faced with a challenge, it's the same steps – take a deep breath and then do it!

Second… We have to believe in ourselves and proceed with confidence. I pride myself in the fact that deep down, I believe in myself. This ability has blessed me and allows me to confidently interact with people all around the world. This is not a skill that I acquired at a young age, nor was easily obtained, but I have constantly worked at it throughout my life and that hard work has definitely paid off.

Small efforts do add up. Every single step we take in the direction of altruistic behaviour makes an impact on our lives and the lives of others. We don't have to make life-altering changes and we don't have to change the world all by ourselves. Oprah had just started her *"Say hi" campaign.* This is one small thing that I have been doing; not only onboard but also everywhere I go, for decades, even in countries where many people don't speak English such as Russia, Norway, Greece, Italy, Turkey, and Portugal etc. How? In some countries, I learned how to say hello in the various languages – not a big task – Bonjour, Ola, Buenos Dias or Guten Tag. Hello is known most everywhere and if that doesn't work, and someone may not understand, then just looking someone in the eye, saying hello with a sincere smile is enough to make anyone's day whether they understand the word or not. I make it a point to look at everyone I pass and greet everyone who makes eye contact with me no matter who the person is. Ninety-nine percent of the time I will get a response in whatever language or at least a smile. If it does nothing else, although most of the time it does, it allows me to walk with my head held high, to confidently face the world and to connect with people. It makes *me* feel good and the interaction not only helps to strengthen my belief in myself, but it also boosts my confidence and leaves me with a firm belief that the majority of people in the world are good and kind.

Third… We must have faith. Having faith does not make everything in life go smoothly or as we wish. However, faith will assist us to pause, breathe and face the challenges as they come, one at a time. Faith will guide us to being present and in the moment, it allows us to do our best, and face our challenges allowing us to move forward. No matter how bad the situation, if we have faith, we will survive and we will move on.

Fourth... Do not resist! Resisting *"what is"* is the cause of our pain and suffering, not the challenge itself. A challenge may be uncomfortable, painful or make us sad but the resistance to it, the questioning why me, why this, why that, is what causes agony. I believe that everything in life happens for a reason and I stand by that belief no matter what challenge comes my way, no matter what I'm faced with or how bad it appears. I believe that challenges make us grow. A key to managing a challenging or stressful situation is to breathe deeply, face the situation head-on, stay present and surrender to it, even when it appears difficult or even impossible; it is just like jumping out of an airplane. We all know deep down from first-hand experiences, that with time – like any storm, this too will pass and the sun will come out again somewhere down the road.

Fifth... Enjoy quiet time. We all need to take the time when we can to experience and enjoy quality me-time, doing what we love or just doing nothing at all, just enjoying "peace and quiet," and slow deep breathing. Not doing so – is again a choice.

Sixth... We have to love ourselves. At a point in my life, not long after quitting smoking, I had a 20-pound weight gain over a five-year period. If you look at it realistically it was a weight gain of four pounds a year and I will confess that before putting on the weight I was very thin. Now all my clothes appeared to be three sizes too small so in my mind I felt that I had to lose a *ton* of weight. My friends thought I was crazy because in their minds I was a healthy weight. For the longest time, I would say, "When I lose the weight I will buy new clothes, feel good and love myself."

I finally had an ah-ha moment, when I got tired of playing that game. I decided that I was going love myself now, exactly as I was at that moment. I chose to go out and buy some new clothes that fit. I continued my attempt to shed those unwanted pounds but with a new *positive* attitude instead of my *wishful thinking and I'll feel better tomorrow* attitude. I also decided that whether I win or lose the battle today I like myself and feel good. Years later, I'm still working to take off those final few pounds, but in the meantime, I love my life, waking up each day, living a healthy lifestyle, attempting to eat well and exercise.

Seventh... Believe in others. If we do not, that alone is a continuous negativity and pain in our lives! We are all human beings, consisting of good, bad, right, wrong, strengths and weaknesses. If we look for the good in people we will find it and if we look for the bad, we will find that as well. Attract the right people into your life. Another lesson I learned was that those who are in our life are there because we choose to let them in. I have said it again and again – I have the most amazing circle of friends, all I have personally chosen. I too, of course, have been chosen by them to be their friend. For those we do not choose, that is okay as well, this world is big enough for us all to cohabitate.

Eighth... Have a positive attitude. Positive people attract positive people and negative people attract, guess what, negative people. I consider myself a positive person; that does not mean that I don't have my moments or even a bad day and that I only have amazing things to say about everything or everyone. When I am thinking negative thoughts I stop and ask myself *"Why am I thinking these thoughts?"* or *"What could I have thought differently"* or even *"What can I do now to turn these negative thoughts around?"*

All negative thoughts can be turned around with some effort. Our thoughts both positive and negative become our actions and our attitude; choose to make yours positive!

Ninth... Just do it! I woke up one day and realized I wasn't accomplishing the things I wanted to accomplish because I was waiting to feel good to feel empowered to do what needed to be done. *Tomorrow I will ...* Those three words gave me the ability to *not do* just about anything that I knew I *should do*. I had *mastered* putting off until tomorrow what I could and should do today. The good news is, now I can see it, acknowledge it and therefore deal with it, by continuing to attempt to take action when I need to, should, or when I consciously choose to. I once read a statement; *suffer for 15 minutes,* which meant, apply 15 minutes to a task you do not want to do, but have to do. Devote 15 minutes without interruption. If you successfully get past the 15-minute mark, you will succeed in completing that task. I tried it and surprisingly it was dramatically less difficult than I had imagined.

Let's face it; if it's not on our minds then it obviously is not important and does not need to be on the to-do list. If it is on the list it will remain an issue until it gets done.

"Just do it!" – Nike

Tenth... Be kind to one another. Thanks, Ellen! It does not cost a thing, it feels good and it works! This is a sentence worth reading again. Another saying I love, *"If you see someone without a smile, give him or her one of yours." – Dolly Parton*

Eleventh... Pay it forward. We need to pay attention to what people do for us. Did someone give you a smile, open a door, let you in line, give you a seat, compliment you, ask you how you are doing etc.? However small a deed may appear to be, we need to get in the habit of doing something nice for someone, we do not even have to know him or her. The world really does work in mysterious ways. We need to stop asking what others can do for us, and start thinking and acting on what we can do for others. Mom and I, years ago, talked about adopting a foster child; we figured that for what most of us spend on coffees in a month, we could assist a child in another country to get an education. At the end of our conversation, we decided not to adopt just one; instead, we decided to adopt one child each! Now we both go through our days knowing that we are assisting two children, one in Egypt and one in Tanzania, who otherwise would not receive this opportunity. Another wonderful thought – imagine if we all could apply the holiday generosity all year round.

Judgment ...

꙳

It started with, "May I join you?" and I responded to his request to sit with me for lunch, "Certainly." He was a handsome young waiter on the ship that I was on during a temporary assignment for three weeks. He was considerably younger, and we ended up having a short-term behind the scenes relationship for the duration of my stay. I am unsure, despite it being a covert relationship, if anyone onboard knew, cared, had an opinion, or a judgment; I did not care. From the moment we are born we are handed rules and morals to live by, this is how we standardize society; you can't, you should not, that is not proper behaviour etc. Because of these societal and shared self-imposed rules and morals we convince ourselves that *we cannot* or *should no*t, even if we want to.

As a society we do need rules and a sense of morality; however, I believe that we should live our lives by our own standards and morals. I was a single adult as was he. I know perceptions have evolved, however, at that time, and even today, it was frowned upon, questioned and eyebrows were raised when the woman is noticeably older than her man. My attitude has always been "Since when is someone's private life anybody else's business?"

I mention this blip in my book solely to bring attention to the judgments we pass based on collective morals and rules. This is just one minor example of judgment as judging others is something that we as human beings do often without even being conscious that we are doing it. We judge people without knowing anything about them or their story. We judge groups because of the actions of a few and it is this judgment that leads to separation, bullying, and unfortunately worse, which is the root cause of fear and hate.

I appreciate the following statement as it really holds true: *do not judge a man until you have walked a mile in his shoes –* American proverb. It may be cliché but it is definitely worth a moment's thought. We don't know what brought others to where they are today, just as others do not know anything about your journey to the here and now. Therefore, we should refrain from passing judgement without knowing the full story and even then, who are we to judge anybody anyway?

Destiny ...

Do you believe that we create our own destiny? Or, do you believe in what was meant to be will be – fate? That was the discussion I had with a wife and husband who were staying in one of the penthouse suites. The woman believed as I did; "*Que sera sera*," her husband, on the other hand, believed you create your own destiny.

I have been fortunate to have experienced many places, people and emotions which have revealed to me that both statements can be true. How is that possible? It is simple; sometimes the choices we make determine our destiny, sometimes we just stumble onto a path! As we make our way on the river or road of life we will come across bends, turns, and obstacles. If you were driving or boating and came upon a concerning bend or obstacle in your path; you would slow down or possibly stop and re-assess the situation. The same applies to life. I believe that these obstacles are placed in front of us, so we can slow down or stop, breathe and re-assess our lives or situations and then make a conscious choice. At times we ignore or drive around the "yellow tape," ignoring the warning signs, thus missing a lesson. Other times we make excuses why we should not stop and re-assess; this may lead to a missed opportunity or causes us to become complacent with our situation. Throughout our lives, we will be presented with choices and those choices determine the outcome of our lives and thus we are deciding our own destiny.

Additionally, I believe that throughout our lives we are given signs that help guide us on our river or road of life. Those signs come in the form of our inner voice, that deep down gut feeling of knowing. An example would be a young child professing that he or she knows exactly what they want to be when they grow up. As life goes by the child is given choices; these choices may take them down a different path for a while. Then those gut feelings re-surface again, directing them to make decisions or a choice that may lead them back to their childhood dream.

I wanted to be a veterinarian when I was young, and a flight attendant and an interior designer. When looking back I note that I have always loved animals, travelling and that I am creative. I began my career as a banker but ultimately it was not where I was meant to be; this was discovered through a series of challenges and choices I was presented with. I continued on that path; I paid heed to the roadblocks, noted the lessons and signs which led me to a choice. The correct choice *at that time* lead me to where I really wanted to be, working on a cruise ship and travelling the world.

I did not pay attention for most of my life, but I now believe that God guides us along the way. Sometimes, we receive a small whisper – some kind of indication; if we ignore it or make the wrong choice, deep down, we know it. The next time, instead of a whisper, He gives us a smack upside the head. If we do not pay attention and ignore it or make the wrong decision once again, next time He hits us with a brick. I came home after one contract and I was so sick with a throat and chest infection that I did not get up off the couch for a week. That lesson was *now you are going to relax and take it easy* and at that point, I did not have a choice – that was the brick! During the course of my life, I have received numerous whispers, smacks and bricks to assist me in learning to pay attention and make correct decisions.

*For every wrong choice that we make along the way,
the Universe is always working to auto-correct,
providing new opportunities again and again
along our path of life, until we get it right!*

Forgiveness ...

I finally understand the term forgiveness and now have the ability to forgive not only others but more importantly myself. Forgiveness does not mean forgetting, condoning, excusing or agreeing with something someone has done or said. Rather, it is the understanding of what has transpired, and having the ability to learn from it and then *let it go*. This goes for what we ourselves may have done, what others may have done, or something that was unjust.

> ***Not forgiving... is like drinking poison***
> ***and expecting the other person to die.***

Throughout my life, I have learned many behaviours, which I believed served well at one time or another, but do not anymore. My life and all that it encompasses, the good and bad, has taught me many lessons, one being forgiveness. I forgive myself for making many bad choices and for hurting myself by not treating my body in the manner in which it deserves to be treated. I forgive myself for engaging in uneventful bad habits for far too long. I forgive myself for all the hours I wasted doing things that didn't assist me what-so-ever in helping me grow as a human being, and for all of my moments of selfishness, stubbornness, and blindness. Through forgiveness I can be truly grateful for all of my newfound wisdom. The wisdom acquired from those mistakes, which I made repeatedly, is what allows me to see things today with an appreciation for all that I am, for all that I am learning and all that I am still striving to be. I can now appreciate that today is a brand new day and if I take care of my body, mind and soul, I can have another one-third of a lifetime to learn, grow and enjoy all that this life has to offer.

By forgiving, we wipe the slate clean and relieve our lives of negative emotions so that we can start our future on a positive note.

Peace...

⹂ℓℓ⹁

"How do you find peace?" That was the question posed to my mom by one of her vacationing friends. It seems that his wife had a negative attitude regarding everything from the weather to the changing neighbourhood. Mom noted her constant negative mood and finally spoke up and said, "You really need to find some peace within."

I thought this was a great question, and it once again led me to a lot of thinking. Life is all about choices; however, what is interesting is that when we have come to that understanding we see everything in a different light. We now have the ability *to choose how* we see life and its challenges and opportunities. Although challenges arise, and when they do our mind may sound off with negative vibes; once we become conscious of the fact that we choose to see things negatively instead of positively we can then start to change those thoughts around. Another one of Tony Robbins famous quotes is, "What's great about this?" When we are faced with any type of negative emotion, like our reaction to rain, for example, we immediately ask the question "W*hat is great about rain?*" If we truly seek for positive answers, they will come. When we sincerely master the art of seeing the beauty around us and live in the moment – we have found peace within.

Laugh...

⁓℮ℓℓ℮⁓

The surprised look on the two male passengers' faces was a sight to behold, so much so that the younger man begged to question me "Where did you come from?" I am not sure if he meant from what country or where did you show up from, because I just appeared and "flew" into the middle seat while the plane was taxiing! I chuckled inside, turned to him and began to tell him my story. I got on board the flight from Rome to Toronto and sat in my assigned seat second row from the back of the aircraft. It was the only aisle seat left when I checked in online and I was the last to board, so when I saw that I had a row to myself, I was grateful; I had a 10-hour flight ahead of me. Just moments after I was seated they came – mom, dad, and a newborn baby! Being the optimistic soul that I am, I prayed that the baby was going to sleep for the next 10 hours but no – it began to cry immediately. The crying did not last for long. However, within a few minutes the parents were having a very long-winded conversation with the flight attendant. I could not make out what was being said since I only know about five words in Italian. Nevertheless, I could tell that they were not happy and it appeared that they did not get what they were promised, whatever that may have been. The attendant went away, came back, they talked some more and then he looked at me, as to ask me a question. I smiled and immediately said, "I don't understand a word." He asked me if I would mind taking another seat to which (hoping of course that I would get a better seat maybe even business class) I immediately said "Certainly." He rushed over to my side, quickly assisted in grabbing all my stuff (bag, computer, books, pillow etc.) and off we went towards the front of the plane. The funny thing about it all was that the plane was taxiing as all this was happening. I was not thrilled with my newly acquired middle seat, and there was nothing that I could do about it. I chose to take a deep breath and reminded myself that *it is what it is.*

The best part of this whole story is that the young man and I talked the entire way home and it turned out to be an incredibly pleasant trip. Alex is his name and he is a wonderful, kind-hearted and very interesting soul. He and I are Facebook friends and I still say that it was truly an honour having the opportunity to have met and befriended him. Everything in life happens for a reason and we might as well make the most of it and enjoy each moment, thus my mantra; live, love and laugh – live in the moment, love the world and those around you and laugh at every opportunity!

Resistance ...

Janice was visiting and the fridge was full. It was time to relax, I had just completed a two-month vacation relief in Europe and I was looking forward to enjoying time with Mom and Janice. I had been home for five days when the phone rang. It was the office asking if I could assist for three weeks, a crewmember had taken ill. I was not excited at the thought of immediately returning to work. However, it was a very good offer financially and more importantly I could not leave the team short-staffed when I was available to assist. Once again, I took deep breath and I informed Janice that I was leaving the next morning. I looked at the fridge full of food, which we had just bought the day before, noticed Mom's expression – she was less than impressed by the whole situation – and once again I had to pack.

Amazingly, that despite all these years of travelling, I still did not enjoy that process of packing; you would think that I would have mastered it – not! In addition, the thought of a second 10-hour flight in one week, just as I was getting over my jet lag, did not sound appealing. All in all, I was not a happy camper, I could feel the resistance within, but I played the *it is what it is* game once again and put one foot in front of the other while compiling a list of positives.

The flight was long but everything went smoothly. It was a long taxi ride to the ship, however a beautiful tour of Istanbul which was followed by an hour and a half wait to pass through customs and immigration before boarding the ship. Once I arrived on board, I got settled in, Mary and I had an amazing dinner out on the back deck with a glass of wine and a spectacular view of Istanbul by night. It was that moment that made me say once again … Life is Good! By 9 pm, despite the ship being docked overnight in Istanbul, I was asleep – I still cannot believe I did that.

Adoration ...

ele

October 2014... I walked up to the departure board at Istanbul Airport. My flight to Toronto was scheduled to depart at 2 pm; I arrived at noon only to find out that there was going to be a five-hour delay. Now I had seven hours to kill which was just another one of life's minor challenges when you travel for a living. I scoped out the airport and then did what I do best; I found myself the most appealing place to have a nice lunch while passing the time with free Wi-Fi. As I was enjoying a lovely bowl of lentil soup while posting my funnies on Facebook, a man and young boy sitting just beyond an arm's length away from me caught my attention. I surmised that the boy was African American and the man was Turkish, I assumed the latter due to his thick accent and us being in Istanbul. I only heard a few words here and there but, eventually, my curiosity got the better of me, as I found this extremely outgoing and energetic young lad very interesting. After a few glances and smiles to and from them both, I finally leaned over, looked at the gentleman and then said to the boy "Excuse me, may I please ask where you're from?" The boy responded, "I'm from Nigeria." "Really," I said, "So what brings you here?" He replied that he was on his way home. I then asked the gentleman, "May I ask what your relationship to the boy is?" I was genuinely interested in how this young boy from Africa came to be there with this man who I thought was Turkish, he said, "He's my son."

As we continued our conversation I learned that the gentleman was Romanian, he had moved to Nigeria many years ago, where his son was born. There was an Ebola outbreak in Nigeria and they thought it best to get away and take a trip back to visit Romania. They had been there for six weeks and were on their way home. The boy's name was Daniel, it turned out that I had a fascinating conversation with them both and at the end of our chat, I said to Daniel "What do you want to be when you grow up?" He said, "I don't know" but then took a napkin, wrote on it and passed it to me. It said, *two years to reach the moon* with a drawing of the earth, a spaceship and the moon. As he was passing me the napkin, I asked him if he by chance was on Facebook, he told me no but then took the napkin back and wrote his email address and phone number. All of this from a 10-year old! I looked at the napkin, chuckled and said, "You probably will reach the moon or maybe develop a cure for Ebola!"

Harmony ...

Can we all live in harmony? I ponder this question often. I find it heartbreaking that in this day and age we are still experiencing so much grief, sadness, pain, atrocities and injustice around the globe. After my grand opportunity of extensively travelling throughout this incredible world, I cannot wrap my head around the fact that so many still do not see people, just as that, as people, one tribe!

Many still choose to see skin colour, religion, sexual preference, brand names, income, real estate, expensive toys and hobbies, just to name a few, as reasons to hate, pass judgment or ostracize. We often look to someone's race, skin colour, religion, sexual orientation, or his or her possessions to form opinions.

We sometimes lack empathy; we choose not to see someone's past, his or her hardships and struggles. Some choose to ignore people living in poverty, war-torn regions, those enduring horrific violence, human trafficking, displaced refugees as well as countless other afflictions both at home and abroad.

We choose to live in fear by not getting to know others for who they truly are; we choose not to trust.

Harmony is when you feel happy. **Harmony** is when people are all getting along. **Harmony** is when people are nice to one another. **Harmony** is the flow of **life**.

So how do we obtain the luxury of living a life of harmony?

I believe to obtain harmony we need understanding + accepting + forgiveness.

1. *Understanding* that we all have different beliefs and different levels of beliefs, which can be positive (constructive) or negative (destructive). We must see all things around us with an empathetic heart and an open mind, understanding that we all see things differently, all from different lenses and that there really is a lot more good than bad in this world.

2. *Accepting* everyone for who they are; the good and bad, what they believe and how they choose to live their life. The world is big enough for us to find and associate with those who share our core beliefs and values.

3. *Forgiveness* is giving up hope that the past could have been any different or letting go of what we thought we wanted. We must focus instead on living in the present moment – the here and now – the only thing we ever truly have. Once we master that, we can move forward – consciously, constructively, lovingly, peacefully and yes, in harmony.

One of the biggest lessons which I am actively working on is to recognize and truly understand that I was not put on this earth to live anyone else's life – only my own! I strive to understand that everyone does not see the world as I do and accept the uniqueness of each person. In addition to my daily gratitude practice, I continue to work hard honing my forgiveness skills, not only toward others but also to myself. If we strive to live our lives by practicing Understanding, Acceptance and Forgiveness we can bring some measure of peace and harmony into our lives and to those around us.

Heartfelt ...

ele

Well, if you have read to this point, I can tell you this; my cards were laid out, my stories told and lessons learned, but not to say, "Hey, look what I did!" Rather, I chose to share with you the experiences of an ordinary girl, and hope that I can inspire the uniqueness in you to shine.

We are all guided to follow our unique individual path in life. Each one of us has greatness within. I believed and listened to that soft inner voice and as it grew to a roar, I responded and found a greatness that is unique to me.

I am grateful for having found the courage to take various major leaps of faith, which in turn have taken my life repeatedly to new levels and experiences. This journey was not without many cuts, scrapes, and bruises as well as a few fractures along the way. These challenges were a result of the times I allowed my mind or my ego to rule me.

My life has been a roller coaster of learning experiences. I have been fortunate to have identified, acknowledged and learned from my life experiences and that of others. I still learn and intend to learn something new every day. I welcome the unknown and the thoughts of taking my life to new levels and experiences in the near future. Today I live in the moment and I am filled with heartfelt gratitude for the life I have been given.

Life is Good... If we really make a conscious effort we can feel and live "life is good" many times a day. Enjoying a cup of coffee, a meal, quality time with someone special or a pet, a nice walk, fresh air, the opportunities are endless *if* we look for them.

Live – Love – Laugh… this has been my Mantra for as long as I can remember. I have it posted everywhere, framed in my room, on my Facebook, under my signature and I truly think that I have maximized living, loving and laughing on all accounts throughout my life.

Live… We need to follow our hearts and do what is right for *us*. What really matters is that you be the person that *you* want the world to see, and aim for whatever *you* want in this life.

Love… is something that I have struggled to learn throughout my life. My feelings about love are different today than they were 30 years ago. At one point in my life, I equated love with marriage and children. Nevertheless, I now know that love comes in many shapes and forms and once we realize that, it really enhances our lives on every level. I am still working hard to make *love* first and foremost in my life.

Laugh… I depend on my sense of humour to get by, and I have used it whenever possible. Some appreciate it and some do not. Oh well, you cannot please everyone. "Life is truly too short not to laugh," and I will say it one more time, "If we don't laugh then the other option is to cry" – take your pick.

Asia ...

◦ℓℓ◦

December 2014... I flew to Australia to catch the ship in Sydney. This contract was once again an educational experience. Our itineraries gave me the opportunity to explore more of Australia than I had previously done, down to Melbourne and over to Tasmania before heading north, up the east coast and then over to Darwin. We subsequently sailed on to Fiji and the South Pacific Islands, including the Isle of Pines, which is the most picturesque island that I have ever seen. It is aptly nicknamed the closest island to paradise; spectacular trees and rock formations, glorious white sand beaches, turquoise water that is so clear that you can see the fishes and coral below. After four days of cruising the South Pacific, we sailed off to Asia. I visited ports of call including Kuala Lumpur, Brunei, Phuket, Dubai, Boracay and Manila. It was the opportunity of a lifetime to experience all of these incredible places for the first time. On this cruise, we also docked in Hong Kong, Singapore, Bangkok, Ho Chi Min City, Bali and more, all ports of call which I had the pleasure to have visited in the past.

Travelling the world is an education in life and in living. My eyes have seen wondrous places and things and I have smiled and dined with people from around the globe. Nevertheless, and of most importance, travelling has given me pieces – pieces of a puzzle, called life. These pieces are the lessons that I have learned. This time around while on my Asian journey my eyes saw different landscapes, not only the beauty of the temples, the many golden Buddha statues, high-end shopping malls, and the architectural beauty of the skyscrapers. A short time and distance away from the financial abundance, you are looking into the eyes of families with children, many living in tiny shacks or on the street. I have seen homelessness here in Canada and elsewhere in my travels, but what stood out in Asia was how prevalent homelessness is. It does not matter where in the world homelessness, hunger and starvation are, there is a real humanitarian crisis, something which we all should be focusing on. The most interesting factor during this Asian cruise was that I learned to see the world through a different lens. Places and things that once I saw through a lens of awe and amazement were now being seen through the lens of my heart.

One of the most notable memories I have is of walking the streets of Manila. During one of my afternoon walks I observed families with children and babies; they were living on the streets and in the parks. I realized something; in acknowledging their existence, I was making a real connection and the feeling was returned with genuine smiles, something I did not expect. Looking directly into the eyes of these beautiful souls you could see the glow of appreciation for the opportunity to be acknowledged and to interact. Even the language barrier did not hinder their joy and excitement. Anything, no matter how little, whether it was money, food or the love and attention from a complete stranger was so truly appreciated. Once again this was a genuine lesson in love and compassion.

Now looking back over my two decades of travel and the interaction with those less fortunate, I see and feel a pattern. Whether at home, or while on the beaches or walking the city streets of the world – people are reaching out to other people; people who are looking for acceptance, attention, assistance and love from another.

When you seriously think about it, this is what we all need and want from each other.

> ***Everyone wants to flourish and everyone wants and needs to be acknowledged and appreciated.***

If we stop and take a moment to be totally present and think about the world in its entirety and what our short time here is truly about; then you can ask yourself *"What does it all really mean to you?"*

Confirmation ...

As things continued to evolve both professionally and personally, I was once again presented with the opportunity to do some major soul-searching. I realized that I had been in my current position for about 15 years and what was once originally a department of one had grown into a department of six people. The company's sales targets and daily operational expectations had gone beyond anything that I could have imagined. I realized, however, that the company's priorities were no longer my priorities; we no longer shared a common goal. I still believed that cruising was an incredible way to travel the world: *"You unpack once and the world comes to you."* Moreover, *"Everyone should cruise at least once in a lifetime,"* and that *"It provides excellent value for your money!"*

However, unfortunately, I had lost my passion for the job. With the increased pressure to sell, my beloved life of working to live became a life of living to work. Additionally, the novelty was waning because most of our itineraries I had experienced on numerous occasions. In addition, with the growing workload, the "see the world" while working on a cruise ship had become more of an occasional luxury.

I finally acknowledged that for all of these reasons I was no longer feeling the passion or loving my life. I was no longer going with the flow of the river. I was instead continually going against the current.

**You can struggle against the current of life
or you can go with the flow.
If you are struggling you are going the wrong way.
Life is not meant to be a struggle.**

In the midst of my recent career challenges and my realization of what was important *to me in my life at that moment in time*,
I once again heard Mom's famous words, "Whatever you do in
your life – make sure *you do* what is right *for you!*" What I did
know was this world was changing rapidly and, therefore, I needed
to assess my own personal situation periodically. I finally got it!
When you are up against your life's challenges you have choices,
you can either work to keep up with the fast-moving carousel that
you are currently on, or you can jump off and find another one
that is more your pace. The same of course would hold true if you
were on a slower moving carousel of life – if you are not content
with your life, you can decide to get off and find the one that is
right for you.

Believe ...

ℓℓℓ

April 19th, 2015... This was the morning I departed my beloved cruise ship for the last time. She was the sixth vessel that I had bid adieu to over the past two decades. Sky Sea Cruises had purchased the vessel and she was en route to dry dock here in Singapore before assuming her new identity as the Golden Era. Many crewmembers stayed onboard, some made their way to other ships and the rest of us were on our way home for vacation.

Miguel and I were departing after midnight so we had the entire day in town before we had to catch our flights. As we were taking a leisurely walk along the beach I decided that I wanted to get my feet wet. While standing knee-deep in water, I looked up and there she was. I was staring back at her for the last time and I realized at that moment that she was about to begin her new and exciting next chapter in life! Suddenly my heart skipped a beat; I took a very long deep breath, and thought, "Could it be possible that I too, may be en route to my next chapter in life?"

She and I had both joined the company within the same month in 1995 and we were about to celebrate our 20-year anniversary. It seriously occurred to me at this moment that I may have been nearing the end of my career on ships! My official anniversary date was coming up in November. This was my goal to reach before retiring, this was the date that I was entitled to the 20-year financial payout, and I realized that I had personally set that goal, that date, for that purpose. I also acknowledged that I could not envision returning to do another contract in order to reach this goal. I was not content enough anymore; my heart was no longer in it. I also realized that this feeling was not born overnight; it had been growing stronger over time.

How on earth was I was going to continue on this path while dealing with these overwhelming dis-eased feelings? How am I going to make it to the finish line? After some more serious soul searching, I had another ah-ha moment! Deep down I knew that despite my challenges in the past, I was continuing to learn and grow. My self-awareness was expanding as was my consciousness, curiosity and interest regarding this glorious world of ours. I wanted, now, not only to see a better world for myself but for *all* the people of the world. Once again I realized that I had arrived at a fork in the road; it was time to make another major change in my life.

I could feel it in my heart. I knew that I was, once again, at that threshold, that very scary step seeing the dream but the reality seeming so far away and not at all within reach.

I was experiencing the exact feelings as I did when I was employed at the bank, having the dream of working on a cruise ship, but no vision of how it could possibly be achieved. I believe that we all come up against these feelings when we have big dreams, which are sadly often followed by feelings or fears that want to stop us in our tracks, causing us to dismiss our dreams. Why do such feelings arise immediately after having these incredible visions?

It may be due to our lack of drive (it is too difficult or I do not know how), or that we choose to stay with what we know and what feels safe. It may be because we fear the unknown or possibly for the worst reason of all, due to our insecurity, our lack of confidence or self-worth, thinking that we cannot, or worse, that we do not deserve to have it. Strangely enough, throughout life I have also feared success, fearing the unknown combined with having to venture outside of my comfort zone. Some just say, "I can't do it," or they listen to other people's opinions, which convince them that they cannot do it – all reasons that bring our dreams to a crashing halt.

Regardless of what issues we are battling, what challenges we personally face or what shortcomings we have in our lives, this *is* what each of our journeys is about; *our* path in life and "*our* Life's Lessons" – doing what is right for *us!*

I had a sudden rush of energy come over me, which did not mean there was no fear, as there was more at that moment than ever in the past. I had just figured out from the Source, my inner voice, my instincts, call it what you will, exactly what I was destined to do with the rest of my life. The solution to my situation was not to beat myself up or claim defeat. The secret to me being successful was to appreciate all that I had experienced, learned and accomplished. The secret to me being successful was to move up that imaginary finish line, to bring my goal within reach. The secret to my success was to proudly step over it, pat myself on the back for a job well done, step forward and take my life to the next level!

Imagine ...

ele

At the completion of the final evening show of the cruise, one of our Cruise Directors gave her farewell speech. She thanked everyone for cruising with us and then said, "If the world could only learn from life onboard a cruise ship! We work with 86 different nationalities all living under one roof in peace and harmony – *just imagine* if the whole world could do that – what a wonderful place this world would be!"

I am still moved when I recall those words. The people, the diversity, the different worlds woven together as one all lead to the reason why I chose to be at sea for 20 years. I was given the opportunity of a lifetime to be a part of this amazing world and without a doubt, those years were a major contribution to my amazing life, so far!

Acknowledgments

∾ele∾

I would like to sincerely thank all who have come into my life; those who influenced me personally and the mentors and coaches who through books, podcasts, summits, YouTube and Ted Talks, all assisted in teaching me a multitude of life lessons.

MOM

You taught me that the most important attributes anyone can have are *the ability to listen and not pass judgment.* You instilled in me how important it is that *we do in this lifetime what is right for us!* In addition, you taught me to *care about others* and *the importance of being there.*

TONY ROBBINS

Through your decades of inspirational teachings, you taught me that *the power we have within ourselves has no limits.*

OPRAH

If you work hard to achieve your heart's desire not only will you achieve it, you will surpass those dreams far beyond what you ever could have imagined! Additionally, *you can do it with the utmost style and grace.*

DR. PHIL
That we can do it all while being genuinely ourselves and with total honesty.

ECKHART TOLLE
For putting it all together in a comprehensible way in both books *"The Power of Now"* and *"The New Earth"* which allowed me to relate to all of this very powerful information that today encourages me to *live consciously and in the moment,* because as you say, *"That is all we have!"*

THE HAY HOUSE WORLD SUMMIT 2014
This sparked my instant fascination with many of the writers and speakers who offered their complimentary yearly podcasts. A special note of gratitude to Dr. Wayne Dyer, who sadly passed away in 2015; his legacy will live on in his book *"I Can See Clearly Now"*, which has had a major impact in my life.

For all that I have been fortunate to have learned thus far, I realize that I have just barely scratched the surface of the wealth of information that is offered in the amazing soul-searching world of Spirituality.

My life has shown me the incredible power people possess in their ability to help change not only their own life but someone else's life; it can be as simple as sharing their own story, and this is why I chose to write *"Twenty Years at Sea, the World as my Classroom."*

And lastly… I would like to say a great big heartfelt "Thank you!" to those who joined me on this creative journey and assisted in creating this gem of a tale. I am ecstatic that I now have the opportunity to share my story with the world… you know who you are – and I love you all!

What's next??

⟨ella⟩

*It is now 2020 ... hmmm!   I am currently working on my next book **... Crossing the Finish Line***

Despite the challenges ... Life is Good!